Linita Eapen Mathew's book t[...]   p
prepare us and make us more sup[...]—[...] [...] shares the experience of so
many who are bereaved who find that: those we believe will support us, don't or
don't know how, many—however well-intentioned—dull their expression of empathy with platitudes, and very few people can cope and stay present with the raw
emotions that are part of loss. Mathew draws out the lonely tendencies of our
individualistic notion of grief in modern western culture, in particular in a society
that is grief-illiterate, which she argues convincingly. This book shows us the what
and the how and supports it with the latest research on bereavement. She teaches
us what we might know about grief to help prepare us and make us more supportive of others, specifically our students. What this book can do for every reader is
remind them that to face grief is to be transformed. To turn away from it is to deny
our humanity and the opportunity to mature into ourselves.

Reinekke Lengelle, Ph.D., author of *Writing the Self in Bereavement: A story of love,
spousal loss, and resilience.*

Dear Soju Uncle & Susan Aunty,

Thank you for supporting our family during our most difficult times. Your acts of love have not been forgotten.
This book is gifted in memory of your lost loved ones. Lovingly, ⟨signature⟩
LINITA.

Life: To Be Given Back Again to Whence It Came

A Pilgrimage Through Prolonged Grief, Confronting Grief Illiteracy and Healing Loss Using the Art of Storytelling

Linita Eapen Mathew

ISBN 978-1-64504-231-0 (Paperback)

ISBN 978-1-64504-233-4 (Hardback)

ISBN 978-1-64504-234-1 (E-Book)

Library of Congress Control Number: 2021952262

Printed on acid-free paper

Cover Image: "The Lovely Woods" by Jayden Kelli @CustomEyesPhotography (Facebook)

This book is part of the Critical Pedagogies Series

DEDICATION

For my first teacher…
as always, for my father, the light of my life.
Eapen Mathew
January 5th, 1946 – January 14th, 2017

The woods are lovely, dark and deep,
But I have promises to keep,
And miles to go before I sleep,
And miles to go before I sleep.
—Robert Frost

'Life

For Most of us it passes – day by day;

Sometimes in pain,

All too rarely with joy,

But mostly it just passes.

Until one day

Our precarious hold slips, is joggled,

and oh-so-nearly falls from our grasp

Then we know, if it's not too late,

That each new day is too precious

Just to let pass.

It is instead a fresh gift given,

To be savoured, whether in pain

Or with joy,

But always to be lived and somehow

To be given back again to whence it came'

—Eapen Mathew, July 6, 1992

ACKNOWLEDGMENTS

I can do all things through Christ who strengthens me.

—Philippians 4:13

For my father, Eapen Mathew, who sacrificed the world and stayed home to alter the course of my destiny, may you know you succeeded.

For my mother, Mary Mathew, who sacrificed staying home and braved the world to secure a good life for her children, may you know you succeeded.

In honor and loving memory of my grandparents: Dr. M.J. Mathew and Mariamma Mathew (paternal) and Mr. Korah Kurian and Annamma Korah (maternal).

***

For my mentors, the guiding lights who led me out of the dark night of grief. Thank you for supporting the work I have set out to do. I am most grateful for your valued contributions to my books: Dr. Thomas Attig, Dr. Reinekke Lengelle, Prof. Aritha van Herk, and Dr. Ian Winchester.

In memory of Dr. Jim Brandon, your encouragement and guidance are ever-present with me.

Table of Contents

Preface

The death of my father destroyed me. Grief was much more than the emotional upheaval I expected it to be—it took away the air from my lungs, the movement in my limbs, the words from my mouth, and toyed with the function of my brain. For three years, I succumbed to a form of complicated grief that crippled me, and no one—*not even me*—could lift me out of my suffering. I was left isolated, alone, and gravely disappointed. I was shattered that he died without a proper diagnosis, and those around me could not bear the weight of my pain nor find the strength to walk beside my bereavement. With my father's loss heavy in my heart, and the injustice of an oppressed, grieving community weighing on my mind, I desired three things: to expand our culture's knowledge on the phenomenon of grief, to bring awareness to our flawed grief etiquette, and to find a way to effectively heal and reconcile with the death of my father. Eventually, I entered the Doctor of Education program at the University of Calgary and set out to explore the large void I had identified in our education system— rifts that contribute to our culture's inability to deal with death, loss, and grief. This book explores three visible gaps of grief and provides one way to move beyond the barrier of bereavement.

Gap 1—Grief Invisibility. As I sat in a dark room, watching my father die slowly, many unanswered questions flooded my mind. Among them, the most sensible arose: *In all my years of schooling, why haven't I been taught how to deal with death?* I had no idea what came next. Naturally, my mind wandered to my students: *How do I prepare them for this? How do I make sure what's happening to me now won't happen to them when the inevitable occurs?* I made the decision, sitting in that chair, to bring grief education into my classroom. But one classroom is not enough. Academically, we have overlooked vital, omnipresent life lessons. We have ignored the importance of embedding grief education into the curriculum, teaching students how to accompany one another through the stressful nature of bereavement, and bringing grief work into the classroom to address the needs of grieving students.

Part I of this book lays the foundation of the significance of this knowledge by intimately exploring the phenomenon of grief, examining well-known grief theories and models more closely, and comparing western and eastern ways of mourning to better understand the transforming effect of rituals on bereavement.

Gap 2—Grief Illiteracy. Because death is universal, our grief-avoidant culture uneducatedly assumes that grief patterns follow suit. Grievers are then stamped and labeled with inaccurate timelines, misrepresentations, and apathetic responses from others—repeatedly, we are told to *get over it*. Quietly, the grieving community hides their pain in the shadows because any form of suffering that is shared is denied. Yet, we cannot necessarily blame others—it is a predisposition of a culture that is forever chasing the joys of happiness, neglecting the meaningful growth acquired from suffering wholeheartedly.

Part II of this book emerged twofold. My autoethnographic study used evocative storytelling to re-create a vivid portrayal of the events before, during, and after my father's death—showing the imprint loss left on me through a collection of 41 stories. Hoping to spark a change, I recount the grief-illiterate actions I endured, shedding light on the dangers of grief illiteracy and narrating the aftermath that insensitive interactions can have on the bereaved.

In Chapter 5 of this book, I deconstruct my autoethnography to support the work of qualitative researchers and those desiring to engage in grief storytelling. However, due to the nature and length of my data, the study itself is published as a companion to this book, titled, *The Revelations of Eapen*. These stories not only evoke emotion but educate, heal, and bring relatability to the reader. Most of all, the companion book, *The Revelations of Eapen*, will resonate with my fellow grievers.

Gap 3—Grief Processing Tools. As I bore the brunt of my sorrow, a societal gap in grief work became clear—that, outside of clinical care, grievers have limited tools at their disposal to move through grief independently and deeply. When my dissertation took form, I approached this issue as both an educational researcher and a griever. I wanted to examine the efficacy of a tool that would be easily accessible to educators willing to support bereaved students. Hence, the overarching question of my study became: *Can written first-person narrative storytelling be used as a tool to actively process and effectively move through grief?* By venturing deep into the distressing aspects of loss and writing out the stories found in the companion book, I began to accept the events of my father's death exactly as they transpired. Intentional storytelling, which leaned on the expressive writing technique (Pennebaker & Smyth, 2016), allowed me to organize my memories, disclose my suffering, and access the positive, benefit-finding aspects of loss—settling my extreme reactions and responses to his death.

Part III provides a thorough analysis of my data by synthesizing grief literature and expressive writing research with the evident themes that surfaced from my stories. Then, I give an overview of student bereavement, addressing the weight of grief on learning. Last, I present my recommendations for educators through a seven-day unit that seamlessly integrates grief work in schools to support grieving students. A cure for loss does not exist, but by using storytelling as a light, we can find our way out of the dark woods and transform our pain into something bearable.

Our level of participation in grief work and finding a vehicle that moves us toward reconciliation is a decision that is ours alone. However, as I witnessed these storytelling strategies successfully help my students process their grief and move through their losses, I realized that we can provide a framework to guide the way as educators. And eventually, as my stories fell into the hands of other grievers, and they shared how simply reading my data brought forward a sense of healing, I understood that my dissertation had already shifted into the concept of these two books. Intentionally, the chapters are written in the first-person narrative to explore grief from a subjective lens, authentically illuminating a vulnerable and hidden topic, death.

The knowledge presented throughout this book is not only a guide for educators, braving to lead grief work in their schools—but also a book of wisdom for the bereaved, mourners searching for answers to soothe their grief. Thus, this book is a manual for the general population (Part I), a companion for the bereaved (Part II), and a toolkit for educators and professional practitioners (Part III).

Above all, this book is the result of the love I carry for my father.

Grief

You came to me

And I hated you

You held onto me

And I pushed back

You forced yourself on me

And I despised you

You tortured me

And I begged you

You isolated me

And I questioned you

You continued to linger

And I learned to live with you

You spoke to me

And I opened up to you

You embraced me

And I embraced you back

You taught me the hard truth

And I softened

But it wasn't until you whispered, I loved him too

That I wept and realized *I loved you.*

References

Pennebaker, J. W., & Smyth, J. M. (2016). *Opening up by writing it down: How expressive writing improves health and eases emotional pain* (Third edition). The Guilford Press.

Definitions of Key Terminology

The key terms relevant to the phenomenon of grief are presented here and will be helpful to keep in mind while navigating through the chapters of this book, bringing context to the material. The verbatim definitions, as explored by grief experts, remain intact.

Acute grief. "A blend of yearning and sadness, with accompanying thoughts, memories, and images of the death and the deceased person, and a tendency to be more interested in this inner world than in the activities that populate ordinary life...[it eventually] becomes integrated, muted, and in the background" (Shear, 2012, p. 120–121).

Bereavement. "The state of having suffered a loss" (Rando, 1993, p. 20).

Choiceless events. "Survivors having little control of death's timing or character" (Attig, 1991, p. 386).

Complicated grief. Also referred to as prolonged or traumatic grief: "This condition is characterized by intense grief that lasts longer than would be expected according to social norms and that causes impairment in daily functioning...complicated grief is persistent, intense longing, and sadness; these symptoms are usually accompanied by insistent thoughts or images of the deceased and a sense of disbelief or an inability to accept the painful reality of the person's death" (Shear, 2015, p. 154).

Grief. "The psychobiological response to bereavement whose hallmark is a blend of yearning and sadness, along with thoughts, memories, and images of the deceased person" (Shear, 2012, p. 120).

Grief reaction. "The full range of our experiences of emotional, psychological, physical, behavioral, social, cognitive, and spiritual impacts of bereavement" (Attig, 2011, p. xxvii).

Grief response. "How we, again as whole persons, actively engage with bereavement and grief reaction emotionally, psychologically, cognitively, behaviorally, socially, and spiritually" (Attig, 2011, p. xxvii).

Grieving. An internal, active coping process after suffering a loss that "requires that energy be invested, tasks be undertaken, and choices be made" (Attig, 1991, p. 387).

Mourning. "The cultural and/or public display of grief through one's behaviours; a vehicle for social communication" (Rando, 1993, p. 23); also, "the array of psychobiological processes that are set in motion by bereavement in order to moderate and integrate grief by coming to terms with the loss and reorienting to a world without our loved one in it" (Shear, 2015, p. 120).

Normal Grief. "Also referred to as uncomplicated grief, encompasses a broad range of feelings, cognitions, physical sensations, and behavioral changes that are common after loss" (Worden, 2018, p. 19).

Reconciliation. "A renewed sense of energy and confidence, an ability to fully acknowledge the reality of the death and a capacity to become re-involved in the activities of living. There is also an acknowledgment that pain and grief are difficult, yet necessary, parts of life...the full reality of death becomes a part of us" (Wolfelt, 2003, p. 146).

Secondary loss. "A physical or psychosocial loss that coincides with or develops as a consequence of the initial loss" (Rando, 1993, p. 20).

Survivor. One who survives: "to continue to function or prosper"; "to remain alive after the death of someone" (Merriam-Webster's Online Dictionary, 2021).

References

Attig, T. (1991). The importance of conceiving of grief as an active process. *Death Studies*, 15(4), 385–393. https://doi.org/10.1080/07481189108252443

Attig, T. (2011). *How we grieve: Relearning the world* (Rev. ed). Oxford University Press.

Merriam-Webster. (n.d.). Survivor. In *Merriam-Webster.com dictionary*. Retrieved May 12, 2021, from https://www.merriam-webster.com/dictionary/survivor

Rando, T. (1993). *Treatment of Complicated Mourning*. Research Press.

Shear, M.K. (2012). Grief and mourning gone awry: Pathway and course of complicated grief. *Dialogues in Clinical Neuroscience*, 14(2), 119–128. https://doi.org/10.31887/DCNS.2012.14.2/mshear

Shear, M. K. (2015). Complicated grief. *New England Journal of Medicine*, 372(2), 153–160. https://doi.org/10.1056/NEJMcp1315618

Wolfelt, A. (2003). *Understanding your grief: Ten essential touchstones for finding hope and healing your heart*. Companion Press.

Worden, J.W. (2018). *Grief Counseling and grief therapy: A handbook for the mental health practitioner*. Springer Publishing Company, LLC.

Foreword

To Grieve, to Speak of Grief

Death comes to meet us when we least expect it, and how we grapple with the pain it brings says much about our humanity. Grief is unpredictable, unaccountable, and impossible to predict or contain. But its eruptive expression makes it uneasy in a world where, for all our age of disclosure, passions are hidden, obscured, or over-complicated. At the same time, we are at the mercy of a culture where too much information can insist on sucking all the oxygen out of tentative moments. Too often, emotions are casually enlisted without thoughtful curation. The perennial, "How do you feel?" is now, regardless of context, a staple query of interviewers and journalists, asked about winning a race or a devastating loss of a family member equally often. The question itself has become so rote, it is starkly unfeeling, to the extent that if anyone were to shout in response, "How the hell do you think I feel?" the reaction would be one of shock. The complacent expectation is that the answer will be subsumed by a cultural reticence that does not recognize the gradations of spirit.

Life: To Be Given Back Again to Whence It Came, and its companion, *The Revelations of Eapen,* Linita Eapen Mathew's acutely personal and moving account of loss and grief, resists and transcends all of these limitations. Raw and effective, her story and its evocative telling enter the fissures between our vague engagement with grief and its genuinely profound experience. Most important, this rendering faces one of the root deficiencies in our contemporary existence: we are uncomfortable with death, and so we cannot fathom grief. We consider anguish a problem to be solved, or a temporary condition that will transpire. Those who mourn are separated and silenced and avoided when they should be witnessed and addressed, not shunted quietly toward a corner.

Grief itself is buffeted by the unsteady apprehension of what matters in emotional realms. As bystanders to another's grieving, we feel ourselves peripheral, voyeurs rather than participants. Because of this unease, we wish it removed or excised like a melanoma; or we turn away with craven heedlessness, fearful that confronting its presence will require what we are not prepared to offer. It is an emotion and experience that we expect others to "get over," possibly the most insulting counsel any person can say to another. Because our culture regards bereavement as a burden, we suffer a common desire to contain and limit that emotion.

We cannot know loss without knowing loss. Death is an abstract until it becomes ours. Mathew aptly encapsulates her father's dying as "an apprenticeship with sorrow." She records in beautiful detail the imprint of that earthquake, and how losing a beloved parent is not a passing ailment but a permanent cicatrix. Her analysis of how grief has been isolated as a malady or disorder unflinchingly identifies one of the shameful deficits of how we live, and in the process offers a new way to encounter and embrace death.

Mathew's autoethnographic approach is poignant and undisguised, mirroring the profundity of her desolation. At the same time, she resists any easy temptation to hyperbolize her trial. The companion, *The Revelations of Eapen*, is thus not a "misery memoir," but instead a document of experience that deepens and enriches the person who encounters grief without ever trying to gloss over the substance of loss. The nature of death and the accompanying natural grief is thus explored as a process and an occupation rather than a passing event; not a phase, but a valuable life repast that must be tasted and even savoured.

This book asks questions that are not asked often enough. Is the language that surrounds grief adequate? Does it embrace the quality of the event and its subsequent reverberation? Does it enable some articulation of death and its complex aftermath, its process, its sufferance, its embrace, and its slow unfolding of acceptance or compromise?

Even our euphemisms are tainted by our fear of death: we refer to the demise of a person in pastel terms: someone has "passed away," or "passed over," or "didn't make it," or is "gone." We send vague messages to family that pretend to express sincerity and sorrow for their "loss," such as "thoughts and prayers," or "thinking of you." It is only too easy to succumb to clichés when we have failed to imagine a language that dares to grapple with the mystery of termination.

The epigrammatic poet J.V. Cunningham sums up our inarticulacy in his poem, "*Consolatio Nova,*" a new consolation.

> To speak of death is to deny it, is
> To give unpredicated substance phrase
> And being.

We do not have the words. And so, as Mathew so effectively dissects, we suffer from grief illiteracy, a terrible lacuna. If we have no language to communicate about death, then we have no language to address other complex passages. And without language, how can we lean into another's grief, with the attention and intentionality that is needed? The tradition of *memento mori*, remembering mortality, must be chronicled, or we lose that invaluable "ability to read the signs written in the texts of our own experiences."

Mathew persuasively argues that stories and the recounting of stories is the best way to negotiate grief, the physical responses of the body to grief, and the effect of intense sorrow on the mind. Through narrative, humans can trace a path between the past and the present, between the inadequacy of language and the profoundly concrete experience of mourning. Stories can supply what is missing, can give shape to the ineluctable determination of absence.

Her book is a remarkable pilgrimage through the landscape of emotions, a threnody for the absence of a dear one, a primer for grief literacy. Her books are also, in Albert Camus' words, a heedful reminder: "Come to terms with death, thereafter anything is possible." They celebrate the need for shared mourning, and they unflinchingly face the power of sorrow as a necessary enablement, one that we must, as a society, offer room and audience for.

Aritha van Herk, CM, AOE, FRSC
Calgary, Alberta

Part I

Telling

Chapter 1

THE INVISIBILITY OF GRIEF

An Introduction

On January 14, 2017, the protective layer of a perceived reality fell to the floor as I entered the world of the grieving community through the devastating loss of my father. At age 31, I was forced to navigate a new and terrifying landscape of life after loss: a life that had no meaning, no flavor, and most of all, little to no support. Walking the path of bereavement, I was falsely reassured that grieving was best done alone, and my inexperience with loss led me to believe them. Because of our lack of education on, and discomfort with, death and grief, I encountered many of the existing misconceptions our society holds toward the grieving process. Hence, three short months after my father's death, the insensitive side of our culture's reaction to grief made itself known. I was told that I had to *move on from him, be grateful for the time I had with him*, and *let him go*. I was bombarded with an outpouring of advice on how to cure my grief, using words that wounded and weakened my spirit. Eventually, the resounding question arose of *how long do you think this will take?* Horrified by the limitations placed on my sorrow, I began questioning my ability to grieve effectively: *Am I ungrateful because I can't 'move on' from my dad? Should it only take four months to grieve the death of a father I had for 31 years?* It was, after all, my first experience with a primary loss: "the death of a parent may be our first significant loss as an adult, so we may have no sense of grief or how to grieve" (Doka, 2016, p. 151). Moreover, it was mostly those who had not experienced a primary loss who were coaching me through my grief, juggling phrases that had little to do with death and more to do with their inability to formulate a language for loss. I quickly learned that—as a culture—we are unable to sit at the table, break bread, stay awhile, and embrace the unanticipated guest of grief.

The Burden of Bereavement in Western Culture

The perception of grief and the reception of the grieving community within the North American context has become a fragile topic. In general, we are a society that encourages positive emotions and discourages or curtails the challenging ones, specifically those revolving around death and public displays of mourning. Our fast-paced culture prevents us from staying present with grief, and the fear surrounding the experience of death adds to our inability to befriend bereavement. Thus, a clear finish line is determined by those close to us, waving a flag to start our journey but unwilling to wait or walk alongside us as we navigate grief's treacherous course. And, if mourning is prolonged, the griever is viewed as *stuck* or *unmoving*; the wildness of grief is only visible to the mourner, who remains caught in its thick entrapment.

Due to the western stigmatization that claims one should not grieve for too long, perfectly normal reactions or responses to the death of a loved one are labeled as unhealthy or viewed as taboo (Cacciatore, 2017; Devine, 2017; Doka, 2016). These unspoken laws suppress the grief of many, causing them to suffer in silence. Yet, bereavement is a crucial and distressing time when the support of one's community, or lack thereof, can either help or hinder one's path to reconciliation (Weller, 2015; Wolfelt, 2014). And still, the human connection required to heal is often removed from the equation. The deeper struggles of loss are not openly discussed, actively processed, or effectively integrated because "there remains a gap in social awareness of the need for bereavement care and the actual practice of providing such services for grieving people" (Breen et al., 2020, p. 2). Instead, grief is ignored, misunderstood, or rushed to disappear, as "our culture sees grief as a kind of malady: a terrifying, messy emotion that needs to be cleaned up and put behind us as soon as possible" (Devine, 2017, p. xvii). The grieving community is then left to find ways to cope with their grief in private, isolated, or small group settings that prevent them from receiving the long-term support needed to navigate the loss of a loved one.

As established by outdated grief theories and models, it is often the other, and not the griever, who ends up dictating what the process of grief should look and feel like: *Maybe you shouldn't talk about him too much; maybe you should get rid of his things or donate his clothes; maybe you shouldn't have so many pictures around, they are reminders* (as if material objects alone can make or break a person's grief). And though the advice or motive behind rushing bereavement may stem from good intentions, any suggestion that removes the deceased from the equation leads the griever onto the path of avoidance or passivity. Which, as Attig (1991) states, amplifies the helplessness of grief,

> The passive concepts of grieving, if accepted by either the bereaved themselves or those who would help, compound, and reinforce these feelings, and encourage and perpetuate the experience and perceptions of passivity at the root of helplessness. They serve to exacerbate rather than alleviate the problem of helplessness. (p. 392)

Accordingly, many myths circulate throughout our communities (Doka, 2016). For example, that grief is predictable, follows a linear timeline, or that we must learn to detach from a loved one and move on—rules that minimize the authentic experience of bereavement and restrict the resources needed to come to terms with life-altering events. When these are the underlying assumptions our culture exudes, the grieving population develops inadequate skills to reconcile with tragedy. And since we are a solution-focused society, grief is frequently medicated and numbed rather than expected to be felt and transformed, as "misconceptions about grief lead more than one million people each year to seek out chemical solutions to their pain, either through alcohol, recreational drugs, or prescription medication" (Doka, 2016, p. 4). We encourage the notion of *curing* grief instead of turning inward and *healing* our losses.

The focus of current grief literature describes what grief looks like, discusses assumptions of how grief will interact with our daily lives, and relays coping strategies through a variety of grief models. However, "conventional models indirectly disempower both the bereaved person and would-be caregivers by implying that grieving people must passively negotiate a sequence of psychological transitions forced on them by external events" (Neimeyer, 2001, p. 165). Although grief is a universal occurrence defined by evolving grief theories and models, advancement in the design of innovative tools that target and teach us how to overcome our suffering has made slower progress, limiting the ways we put these theories and models into practice. The scope of literature that deals with processing loss through actively grieving (Attig, 1991) is somewhat static, and the exercises created to mourn independently usually only provide short-term relief. Devine (2017) posits that "there's a gap, a great divide between what we most want and where we are now. The tools we currently have for dealing with grief are not going to bridge that gap" (p. xvii).

A lack of rigorous techniques combined with our unwillingness to deconstruct the impact of grief hinders our ability to effectively integrate and move beyond our suffering. Thus, it is crucial to raise our awareness around the true, subjective nature of the grieving process and develop groundbreaking methods of healing that support grief work and survivor reconciliation. And to strengthen the tools and interventions needed to move beyond grief, we must first learn how to lean into it.

A Lack of Language for Loss

Whenever a social media post announces the loss of a loved one, I immediately move to write something comforting: *Dear _____, my thoughts and prayers are with you and your family at this time.* I hit the post button, and a sense of relief can be felt that I did my part. But upon scrolling through the rest of the condolences, it becomes glaringly evident that the bereaved person's wall is overflowing with mirroring messages: *my thoughts and prayers are with you, thinking of you and your family during this difficult time, my sincere condolences, sending love and healing,* and so forth. Basic phrases stored away in our minds are brought out and delivered at the crucial time of loss, whether in-person or online.

Stepping back, I realized that I, too, struggled to construct an authentic language for loss—that our evasive culture had not encouraged me to learn meaningful discourse that genuinely supports another's deep grief. Not only at the beginning of one's bereavement, but throughout, we resort to using platitudes and clichés. Yet indifference is not the issue, we do care, we simply do not have the language to express our feelings on loss without pretense. To change *I can't imagine what you're going through* to sound more like *I will try to imagine and honor your loss* requires empathic mind work, using intentionally chosen wording. Moving beyond the expressions that make up our standard condolences—constructing a language of grief—takes time, effort, and careful deliberation of our words. Our poor construction of a language for loss is understandably not our fault; we are not explicitly taught the literacy of grief.

The Sting of Grief Illiteracy

Everyone dies. Two words that cause the mourner rolling the weighted boulder of grief up the mountain of bereavement to slip, lose their grip, and get toppled over. The shortest phrase in the English language that evokes the most damage—shaming, belittling, stifling one's grief—is typically said by those who have not experienced a toppling-over-type of loss. Everyone does die, and still, I never believed death would target my family. Assassinated by his loss, my father's blood spilled through my raw wounds, mortifying those around me. And, because "we are a grief-illiterate nation" (Shriver, 2014, p. xi)—*well, everyone dies*—were the chosen words used by others hoping to remedy my suffering.

My desire to study the phenomenon of grief arose after being confronted with the alarming rate of grief illiteracy in North American culture. Although the term *grief literacy* has garnered attention in today's vernacular, as we now deal with multiple forms of grief materializing simultaneously from these pandemic circumstances, I have yet to find a source that clearly defines what grief illiteracy is. And since I argue that the latter concept creates a more pronounced understanding of our need for grief education in schools, as most of us are disadvantaged, I would like to take a moment to unpack this term. If Merriam-Webster's (2021) online dictionary defines *grief* as "deep and poignant distress caused by or as if by bereavement" and *illiteracy* as "the state of not having knowledge about a particular subject" then, grief illiteracy can be summed up as the state of not knowing the deep distress caused by death. And, if we were to travel beyond the simple derivation of the term and stretch inward into our intellectual, emotional, and spiritual reserve, the following conversation appears:

> *Grief illiteracy* refers to the individual, communal, or cultural lack of education and empathy about the deep distress caused by death (or non-death) losses. *Grief literacy* implies both cognitive knowledge about mourning and attachment, as well as empathy toward self and others, allowing the bereaved to become better connoisseurs of the deeply unwelcome transition of loss. As

socially situated, dialectical and dialogical beings, this requires an openness to our own emotions and meanings as well as to those of others, supported, opposed, or unseen in a broader relational web, drawing on the (always constrained) resources of our tribe, place, and time in recognizing, articulating, and negotiating the significance of these experiences. Simply stated, grief literacy implies an ability to read more deeply the significance of our own emotions, making sense of the personal and relational needs implied by them. (L. Mathew, R. Lengelle, & R. Neimeyer, personal communication, May 12, 2021)

Throughout my bereavement, my eyes were forced open to see that grief is treated much like the untouchable caste within the emotional hierarchy; many are unable to interact with another's grief using deep sensitivity. In 1961, C.S. Lewis spoke honestly following the loss of his beloved wife, Joy, when he wrote, "Perhaps the bereaved ought to be isolated in special settlements like lepers. To some I'm worse than an embarrassment" (p. 11). And yet, sixty years after his observation was made, the sentiment remains unchanged for those of us who grieve. *Still*, our lack of education on the phenomenon of grief negatively impacts the grieving community.

As I moved through my father's death, these detrimental challenges fueled my desire to better understand the grieving process on both a personal and academic level. Six months into my grief, I began reading current grief literature to make sense of what was happening in my cultural context. I joined grief support groups and observed a common theme among members who felt like outcasts within society. To sit and hear similar stories not only brought the extensive repercussions of grief illiteracy to light, but my awareness grew around the alleviating effect of telling stories—of expressing our shared lived experiences (Bochner & Ellis, 2016). Slowly, a need for change began to brew. Bewildered by the grief illiterate actions of others, and being a teacher through and throughout, the understanding dawned on me that the only way to combat grief illiteracy is to increase our knowledge on the subject matter: "a grief literate society will only occur as an outcome of education and action" (Breen et al., p. 6, 2020). Ignorance can only be defeated by a consistent and deliberate implementation of an education on grief.

The Gap of Grief Work in Schools

When I entered the doctorate program, I set out to explore the gaps I had identified in our education system—that grief education and grief work are nonexistent in schools, leaving grieving students raw with their wounds. Lately, terms and phrases such as *wellness, well-being, self-care strategies*, and *proactive mental health* are trending in staff meetings and professional development sessions. However, bereavement—a time when this attentiveness is needed most—is still being swept under the rug. James and Friedman (2009) support that "we are far better prepared to deal with minor accidents than we are to deal with grief. We receive more education about simple first aid than we do about death, divorce, and other emotional losses" (p. 23). Thus, the current state of our education system is reinforcing the notion that we are a culture that avoids dealing with intense pain, bypassing the need to make space for this vital work instead of facing it head-on. Simultaneously, a societal gap arises—that mourners have little guidance on how to process their grief independently outside of clinical care, a pivotal issue I empathized with. A new perspective, a shift away from cultural and academic neglect, is required to close the current knowledge gap.

Unaddressed student grief can lead to dire consequences as adolescents who are not taught how to self-regulate through distressing life events have a higher chance of participating in at-risk behavior (Cohen et al., 2017; Van der Kolk, 2014). And for some, chronic grief is an indicator of long-term mental health illnesses: "an estimated 11% develop the mental health disorders of complicated grief (CG) and depression" (Ghesquiere et al., 2015, p. 2173). If interventions specifically targeting bereavement are not introduced in schools, festering and unprocessed grief could further contribute to the decline of students' overall well-being and quality of life, increasing the rate of poor mental health statistics rising within our school systems (Kutcher et al., 2015). The impact of student bereavement and the challenges grief brings into the classroom are more largely discussed in Chapter 7.

As educational leaders, the language we use to address the grieving community matters. Those in leadership roles should never expect staff or students to get over their loss in days, weeks, or months. By using grief-illiterate language, leaders express to those in their care that their story does not matter—the story of their deceased loved one does not matter. To reconcile with tragedy takes dedicated stamina and endurance that, in my own experience, even with the excessive amount of grief work I did, required a minimum of three years to break the shell of my sorrow. And to complete grief work effectively—space, time, and constant and consistent support are non-negotiable. Since students spend most of their time in schools, we are best positioned to ensure their loss is witnessed and processed. We can no longer ignore the crisis in our midst by passing the problem on to clinical care workers, hoping they will douse the fire intensifying in our buildings, especially when we have competent educators and our own supply of water.

Hence, I am advocating on behalf of my students for a tool to be introduced in schools that will allow them to actively work through, process, integrate, release, and heal from severe losses. As an English teacher, I know students are already attracted to writing through their emotions; it is a tool easily accessible within the four walls of a classroom. Thus, this book raises teacher awareness on how to intentionally incorporate therapeutic writing techniques into their task design, effectively supporting student bereavement and addressing grief in schools. With careful regulatory structures in place, storytelling that uses expressive writing techniques can be used as a tool to help grieving students process their pain.

Writing Out the Weight of Grief

A tool that is gaining recognition in grief literature today is brief, expressive writing exercises, "a technique where people typically write about an upsetting experience for 15 to 20 minutes a day for three or four days" (Pennebaker & Smyth, 2016, p. ix). Communicating our emotions is a natural reaction to stressful life events, and expressive writing researchers determine how the writing should be constructed and in which circumstances written narrative strategies are most successful, maximizing the potential of this technique (Leopore & Smyth, 2002; Pennebaker & Evans, 2014; Pennebaker & Smyth, 2016). A more thorough review of expressive writing literature, and these findings, will be discussed in Chapter 6.

Since I was a little girl, writing has always been my chosen avenue to work through difficult situations and find healing. Over the years, I have kept diaries, journals, flash drives, and even loose sheets that

I scribbled on to get my thoughts out on paper. The physical act of writing and connecting my intense emotions to language provided catharsis from traumatic experiences I had faced, opening a passageway toward meaningful transformation. Thus, it was no surprise that when my father died, I found pockets of release from disclosing my pain through writing. First, I wrote his eulogy and then his obituary; that writing combined with ritual practices somewhat dulled the immediate sharp, piercing pain. Then, without hesitation, I wrote letters to my father so that he would not miss a moment of my life, a tradition that remains intact. And, eventually, I embarked on the journey of completing my doctorate, where I committed to writing a series of short stories that narrated, to the best of my ability, my father's final weeks on earth—stories that are shared in the companion book.

Autoethnography as a Methodology

Autoethnography—"an autobiographical genre of writing and research that displays multiple layers of consciousness, connecting the personal to the cultural" (Bochner & Ellis, 2016, p. 65)—became a vehicle for me to examine my severe reactions and responses to loss. Because of the paralyzing nature of my grief, I knew I would be able to provide rich narratives describing my inner experiences as one of the goals of autoethnography is to bring "heightened attention to human suffering" (Bochner & Ellis, 2016, p. 45). By reflecting on my story of loss, it became clear that the most effective way to confront cultural grief illiteracy was through revealing my own challenges with bereavement and discovering myself *first* in the context of grief.

When investigating a phenomenon that deals with the human condition, my task as the researcher was not only to inform the audience about the topic, but to engage, perform, mirror, interpret, and provoke epiphanies that accompany the experience of grief (Denzin, 2014; Holman Jones et al., 2013). Embracing my vulnerability as the subject and reclaiming the power of insider knowledge allowed me to intimately explore the effect of writing on bereavement, and act as a mirror for others, giving voice to the larger, often muted, grieving community. Using evocative autoethnography, written to evoke emotion in the reader by allowing "the story to do the work" (Bochner & Ellis, 2016, p. 60), I wrote out an in-depth account of my loss through 41 stories that shed light on the cultural impact that social interactions played on the development of my grief. By design, I took the expressive writing technique (Pennebaker & Smyth, 2016) and expanded upon its guidelines using the art of storytelling to decipher whether extensive, structured narrative writing would effectively process the pain of losing my father. It was through this method of storytelling, initiated almost two years after his death, that I finally began integrating his loss and felt a more substantial shift toward reconciliation.

Storytelling as a Method

Storytelling has always infused itself into my life. My father, an English teacher, approached our education through stories, whether through the fables he told my brother and me before bed or the life lessons he summarized through a tale of his own. He taught me to see and interpret the world using stories because for some, including myself, "narrative and storytelling, are crucial ways of knowing" (Holman Jones et al., 2013, p. 31). Later on, this narrative power extended into other areas of my life, such as performing folklore through Indian classical dance, honing my skills as a writer, or pursuing my own career as an English teacher, instilling my love of storytelling in students. As Bochner and Riggs (2014) explain,

> Our lives are rooted in narratives and narrative practices. We depend on stories almost as much as we depend on the air we breathe. Air keeps us alive; stories give meaning to our existence. They become our equipment for living. (p. 76)

Perhaps this was another reason why my father's death affected me so deeply. Shortly after he died, I felt his story slipping away, becoming blurred, forgotten, and for some, erased. Holding onto my father's story became necessary for my survival, and so I started reshaping it. I began to believe if they remembered his truth or had greater insight into the depth of our relationship, they would try harder to keep his memory alive—or at least form empathy for my grief. And within my hands, I held a powerful tale of love, loss, and grief that was relatable and could be told well. Eventually, I realized that if I crafted my words carefully, drawing out the universal components of loss, a great storyteller reaches an audience grander than social circles. Culturally, if the stories of our losses are laid bare, grief would have room to breathe.

Storytelling that uses rich, figurative language to describe abstract thoughts and emotions may help assimilate an event more effectively than speaking through literal terms that do not match the severity of the loss (Pennebaker, 2000). Neimeyer (1999) states that "a well-chosen narrative method may prove to be a powerful means of articulating and addressing loss in such cases precisely because written self-expression is a novel experience" (p. 71). And as previous studies have shown, the bereaved found sharing stories of the deceased to be more helpful than professional counseling (Castle & Phillips, 2003).

For close to a year, I consciously engaged in grief work by immersing myself in creating grief narratives for my study as "autoethnographic stories attempt to bring vivid and resonant frames of understanding to one's anguish and pain" (Bochner & Ellis, 2016, p. 69). Due to the novel nature of these 41 stories, they do not appear in this book. Instead, my data is published separately as a companion to this manual. Here, I gathered information from multiple sources, organized the events in chronological order, and wrote out the fine details of my father's death in over two hundred pages. I envisioned my data would create identifiable categories, observations, or rationales that would lead to insightful conclusions that would support the grieving community as a whole. And, at the end of my rigorous, painful, and awakening study—I was *right*. I determined that structured, first-person narrative writing was a successful tool used to recover from, reconcile with, and integrate the loss of my father. Now, I want to share my analysis with others to help lift the heavy boulders of grief off the shoulders of the bereaved.

A Companion for the Bereaved

Whenever I picked up a book written on grief, what held great value for my healing, more than the author's profession or academic credentials, was their intimate understanding of loss through their own significant encounter with the death of a loved one. *Are they trustworthy to lead me out of the thick fog of grief?* Or, are they speaking from a third-person perspective that lacks a dimension of depth to the actual cruelty of bereavement? As Bochner (1997) reveals,

> I had studied, theorized, and taught about loss and attachment for more than two decades, but I had to admit that I didn't really begin to *know* loss until I experienced my father's death. And the more I thought about my own experi-

ence of loss, read other people's accounts of loss, and reviewed the theoretical and research literature, the more I began to understand that the academic world was not in touch with the everyday world of experience, the ordinary world. The research literature offered me data, labels, categories and theoretical explanations, but it didn't express how loss felt and it didn't invite engagement with the particularities of the experience. (p. 424)

The underlying rationale for this book is to invite readers into how loss feels—wholly and entirely. Some may benefit from the research offered here, some from the stories found in the companion book, and some from storytelling through their own sadness—I invite you to read the parts that call to you. And for the grieving hearts whose hands have found their way to my books, I have traversed the dark wooded path of grief, nearly succumbed to its terrain, but somehow found my footing and survived. This manual explores the *somehow* bearing gifts for those who grieve, hoping to find relief.

My Worldview

To more deeply understand my journey through bereavement, I must first describe my duality. I am a second-generation Canadian raised with both Indian and Canadian values, two worldviews pooled into one. My parents immigrated from Kerala, India, and out of their combined 14 siblings, they were the only two to leave the Asian continent. On July 3, 1975, my mother took a risk and traveled to Canada to work as a registered nurse in Newfoundland. And, in November of 1978, my father, with whom she was engaged through an arranged marriage, followed her here. They were married in St. Anthony, Newfoundland, on December 2, 1978. Two years later, my brother was born in Halifax, Nova Scotia, and in search of work for my father, they settled in Calgary, Alberta, where I was born.

Because of my unique cultural hybrid, I can examine bereavement and the societal implications from an eastern and western perspective. The values and ideations of both cultures add to the integrity of the self-study I conducted on grief. The logical mind work springs from my formal western education; however, the intuitive erudition of the nature of being and suffering rises from the depths of my eastern roots. As a grief researcher, I felt it was important to provide a glimpse into the challenges we faced as an ethnic family immigrating to Canada, and thus, a clearer understanding of the close and irreplaceable bond developed between a father and his daughter.

My Relationship with my Father

Although I was fortunate to be brought up with two loving parents, my father raised me. In more ways than one, he was *my best friend*. Being highly sensitive and introverted, we had a subtle soothing energy that calmed one another. With him by my side, I knew I would stand undefeated against the perils life handed me—and life handed me many. Thus, when he died, I became vulnerable to genuine suffering; a loneliness I had never felt before suffocated me and smothered my will to live. As Doka (2016) suggests, "even though losing a parent is a near universal loss, we are never fully prepared for the effects a parent's death can have on us. We can be orphaned even as adults" (p. 151). Yet, his demise was not extraordinary. It was very much the ordinary, everyday loss encountered by most of us. As some would say, it followed the natural order of life—and still, it felt unnatural. His final moments were not exotic nor painted as overly tragic or traumatic—and still, they traumatized me. His loss should have been expected and thus less painful—and still, it was startling and agonizing. Truly, it was a *perfect* death—and still, it crippled me to my core. Losing my father ripped me open from head to toe and rearranged everything inside me, leaving me a completely different person altogether. I viewed the love between a father and daughter as a *once-in-a-lifetime* love. Hence, as much as I consider the type, cause, and order of death to be critical factors that contribute to the intensity of one's suffering—throughout this book, I emphasize the bereaved person's relationship to the deceased, and their perception of that bond, as the most important ingredient in the recipe of one's grief.

My father was a highly educated man; he held the highest academic credentials on both sides of the family—the only person to surpass him was me. He was an English college lecturer who traveled to Canada to be with my mother, bringing the hope of completing his doctorate in a North American institution. Unfortunately, in the late seventies, his former three degrees were not recognized here. He attempted to start his education over, but with the high cost of living and caring for two small children, he settled on completing a diploma in computer programming to earn a living, leaving his vocation behind.

Yet, confronted with the barriers of racism and a recession, my father only remained employed for short periods. In time, he accepted his role as a househusband, a life-altering decision that forced him to surrender a life that could have been. Dad was quiet, reserved, and shy—a person who, I have come to understand now, probably struggled with feeling emotions as deeply as I do. And, to accept the transition from his hopes and dreams to those of his children, he turned inward and found the spiritual meaning behind his suffering. Knowing that his sacrifices would benefit my brother and me, he moved forward with only us in mind. He was an honest, genuine, dedicated, and extremely loving father, raising both of his children to the best of his ability. And still, culturally, his decision was not accepted; I witnessed his harsh reality. Even now, the comments *echo* long after his death.

My mother often reminisces how since she was our sole provider, she had to return to work a mere two months after I was born. She placed me in my father's arms, and the only time he let go of me was when he died. My father shaped my world; my values and understanding of life come directly from him. Throughout my years, I fought to give value to his life. I experienced his mind intimately, and I knew he was brilliant. But because he did not earn a set salary, others often overlooked the strides he was making—his unwavering dedication to his wife, children, religious teachings, and city-wide volunteer work. I became overprotective of him and did my best to shield him from ignorant and insensitive comments. For instance, in my first year of university, I wrote a paper in my sociology class about the cultural criticisms that househusbands face—it was the only paper I received an A+ on that year. Thus, whenever my passion springs from the love I have for my father, my soul knocks on the door of success. My attachment to him—my primary caregiver—constructed my grief, and as Parkes and Prigerson (2010) note, "when one person greatly relies on or has a strong…attachment to another the severance of the relationship is likely to give rise to difficulties" (p. 165). At the center of the layers upon layers of stories that formed the potency of my prolonged grief, existed him. Still, he continues to be the most influential person in my life.

When I was 19, my father suffered a silent heart attack and watching him lie in a hospital bed on the brink of death changed the direction of my career. On a whim, I decided I would fulfill his lifelong dream of teaching and completing a doctorate in this country. It was more of an immediate response reaction, and no conscious planning or thought was given to the decision. Yet, as I moved into teaching, this profession felt more aligned with my spirit, a path where I felt more at home. And the doors of education opened with ease and grace as though a *divine* shift had occurred. When revisiting and confronting this decision later on in my Master's degree, I realized how suffering had placed me on the path of my vocation. And soon, yet again revolving around my father, suffering would place me on higher ground.

At 31, I came face-to-face with my father's death. Being part of a low, single-income household throughout my formative years, we had very little, but we did have each other. A small family of four, the isolation of being away from our extended family caused us to rely heavily on each other. However, an unexpected and unknown illness suddenly shook our lives when my father's health rapidly declined. Shulman (2018) supports that traumatic loss does not only stem from violent circumstances; it can also arise when "someone who is integral to our identity dies following illness" (p. 86). And so, when the strongest pillar eroded, the rest of our house collapsed. His death was an earth-shattering experience. Yet I remember sitting in the hospital awaiting the fate of my father, asking myself, *why now?* "Before you tell your life what you intend to do, listen for what it intends to do with you" (Palmer, 2000, p. 3). Internally, I heard a strong voice, a knowing, a rebuttal: *why not now?* It was then that my suffering created a spiritual opening of surrender and acceptance. My years of preparation, my formal education, my intuitive wisdom, and my contemplative, spiritual understanding of life—all joined forces to give me a solid answer. The time had come, both his and mine, to evolve to a higher state. And, with his last breath, my pilgrimage through prolonged grief began.

In my eulogy, I referred to my father and myself as twin flames, one soul, contained in two bodies. I look like my father, think like my father, talk like my father, write like my father—and I even became a teacher just like my father. My sense of self confidently rested on his shoulders. Hence, when those shoulders that carried me so steadily for 31 years were suddenly removed from out under me, my identity—like our family system—shattered. The intensity of my grief was so severe and my suffering was so prolonged that, truly, I was unsure of my fate. Darkness pervaded my existence, chances of recovery seemed bleak, and yet, still, I knew on a spiritual level something was brewing: "Sometimes in your darkness you may sense that something is incubating in you or that you are being prepared for life. You are going somewhere, even though there are no external signs of progress" (Moore, 2004, p. 4). My father taught me to find the root of my suffering to work through and heal my pain. Thus, cultivating a deep and rigorous awareness of my internal landscape was the only way for me to restore balance and achieve a peaceful mindset amid severe distress. It is safe to say that I had to do the mind work to find healing—and the mind work I have done will greatly benefit the narratives written throughout this book.

Organization of the Book

This book opens a door to bereavement, offering a firsthand account of the anguish of loss.

Part I: *Telling*—The first section of this book educates readers on the phenomenon of grief, summarizing and reframing current grief literature against my reactions and responses to my father's death. By telling the physical, social, psychological, behavioral, and spiritual impact of prolonged grief, I provide a comprehensive and detailed account of the toll the death of a loved one can take on a person's whole being. Using a subjective lens, I narrate the evolving relationship between grief and griever, the multidimensional aspects of mourning, and the consequences one's cultural context can have on bereavement. Next, I explore the impact of grief work by closely investigating four popular process models, relaying how each interacted with my grief and influenced my reconciliation. Last, I give insight into a second, eastern perspective of mourning, sharing how Indian Christians grieve, highlighting the healing power of ongoing death rituals and the long-lasting result of communal grieving.

Part II: *Showing*—The centerpiece of my doctoral study was my evocative autoethnography, *The Revelations of Eapen*, a collection of 41 real, raw, and vulnerable stories I wrote to reconcile with the loss of my father. The tears I shed recounting these tales were innumerable but spilled with intent. I wrote one draft, *it was not enough*; I wrote a second draft, shape took form; I wrote a third draft, the story was whole; I wrote a fourth draft, a book emerged. As such, Chapter 5 of this book deconstructs my autoethnography, inviting readers into my storytelling process before reading the analysis of my data. However, as previously mentioned, the showing of grief—the autoethnographic data itself—is presented uniquely as a companion to this book, as the stories evolved organically on their own. Gladly, I open and reveal the depth of my brutal wounds, drawing readers into the core of my heart. All I ask of those choosing to read the companion is to approach with reverence for what lies at the center—*my beloved father*.

Part III: *Synthesizing*—The goal of my study was to investigate the potential of using storytelling as a tool to actively heal and effectively move through grief. Hence, Chapter 6 explores the scientific knowledge of trauma's effect on the brain, previous expressive writing research, and the analysis of my data—blending knowledge from all three sources to refine a tool that targets bereavement. In Chapter 7, I examine student bereavement statistics in Canadian schools and discuss how grief might materialize in the classroom, interfering with the personal and professional lives of students. Using the findings from my autoethnography, I present my recommendations on how to bring grief education and grief work into the classroom, supporting bereaved students through a seven-day unit plan entitled, *Storytelling Through Your Sadness*.

As an educational leader, the maximized potential benefit of my book would be to lead a *Grief Revolution* where communication, compassion, and companioning grief (Wolfelt, 2006) becomes embedded within our pedagogical practice. Often people ask me, *how do I prepare for grief?* We prepare for grief by preparing our communities to companion grief effectively. This revolution needs to take place within the education system because here lies the responsibility to teach, train, and ready students for success in life. And yet, we continue to leave grief education out of our curriculums—we continue to set our students up for failure when navigating an inevitable, universal aspect of humankind, death. Therefore, I aim to invoke a cultural shift where the invisible becomes visible. A breakthrough where bereavement is embraced and the grieving community is encouraged to actively grieve and consciously move through life's most difficult and trying time—the death of a loved one.

References

Attig, T. (1991). The importance of conceiving of grief as an active process. *Death Studies*, *15*(4), 385–393. https://doi.org/10.1080/07481189108252443

Bochner, A. P. (1997). It's about time: Narrative and the divided self. *Qualitative Inquiry*, *3*(4), 418–438. https://doi.org/10.1177/107780049700300404

Bochner, A. P., & Ellis, C. (2016). *Evocative autoethnography: Writing lives and telling stories*. Left Coast Press.

Bochner, A. & Riggs, N. (2014). Practicing narrative inquiry. In P. Leavy (Ed.), *The Oxford handbook of qualitative research* (pp. 195–222). Oxford University Press.

Breen, L. J., Kawashima, D., Joy, K., Cadell, S., Roth, D., Chow, A., & Macdonald, M. E. (2020). Grief literacy: A call to action for compassionate communities. *Death Studies*, 19. https://doi.org/10.1080/07481187.2020.1739780

Cacciatore, J. (2017). *Bearing the unbearable: Love, loss, and the heartbreaking path of grief*. Wisdom Publications.

Castle, J., & Phillips, W. L. (2003b). Grief rituals: Aspects that facilitate adjustment to bereavement. *Journal of Loss and Trauma*, *8*(1), 41–71. https://doi.org/10.1080/15325020305876

Cohen, J. A., Mannarino, A. P., & Deblinger, E. (2017). *Treating trauma and traumatic grief in children and adolescents*. The Guilford Press.

Denzin, N. K. (2014). *Interpretive autoethnography* (Second edition). SAGE.

Devine, M. (2017). *It's ok that you're not ok: Meeting grief and loss in a culture that doesn't understand*. Sounds True.

Doka, K. J. (2016). *Grief is a journey: Finding your path through loss*. Atria Books.

Ghesquiere, A. R., Aldridge, M. D., Johnson-Hürzeler, R., Kaplan, D., Bruce, M. L., & Bradley, E. (2015). Hospice services for complicated grief and depression: Results from a national survey. *Journal of the American Geriatrics Society*, *63*(10), 2173–2180. https://doi.org/10.1111/jgs.13656

Holman Jones, S. L., Adams, T. E., & Ellis, C. (2013). *Handbook of autoethnography*. Left Coast Press, Inc.

James, J. W., & Friedman, R. (2009). *The grief recovery handbook: The action program for moving beyond death, divorce, and other losses including health career, and faith* (20th anniversary expanded ed.) Collins Living.

Kutcher, S., Wei, Y., & Morgan, C. (2015). Successful application of a Canadian mental health curriculum resource by usual classroom teachers in significantly and sustainably improving student mental health literacy. *The Canadian Journal of Psychiatry*, *60*(12), 580–586. https://doi.org/10.1177/070674371506001209

Lepore, S. J., & Smyth, J. M. (Eds.). (2002). *The writing cure: How expressive writing promotes health and emotional well-being*. American Psychological Association.

Lewis, C. S. (1961). *A grief observed*. Bantam Books.

Merriam-Webster. (n.d.). Grief. In *Merriam-Webster.com dictionary*. Retrieved November 11, 2020, from https://www.merriam-webster.com/dictionary/grief

Merriam-Webster. (n.d.). Illiteracy. In *Merriam-Webster.com dictionary*. Retrieved May 12th, 2021, from https://www.merriam-webster.com/dictionary/illiteracy

Moore, T. (2004). *Dark nights of the soul: A guide to finding your way through life's ordeals*. Gotham Books.

Neimeyer, R. A. (1999). Narrative strategies in grief therapy. *Journal of Constructivist Psychology*, *12*(1), 65–85. https://doi.org/10.1080/107205399266226

Neimeyer, R. A. (2001). *Meaning reconstruction & the experience of loss* [Kindle version]. Retrieved from Amazon.com.

Palmer, P. J. (2000). *Let your life speak: Listening for the voice of vocation*. Jossey-Bass.

Parkes, C. M., & Prigerson, H. G. (2010). *Bereavement: Studies of grief in adult life, fourth edition*. Penguin Books.

Pennebaker, J. W. (2000). Telling stories: The health benefits of narrative. *Literature and Medicine*, *19*(1), 3–18. https://doi.org/10.1353/lm.2000.0011

Pennebaker, J. W., & Evans, J. F. (2014). *Expressive writing: Words that heal*. Idyll Arbor, Inc.

Pennebaker, J. W., & Smyth, J. M. (2016). *Opening up by writing it down: How expressive writing improves health and eases emotional pain* (Third edition). The Guilford Press.

Shriver, M. (2014). Foreword to the anniversary edition. In Kübler-Ross, E., & Kessler, D., *On grief and grieving: Finding the meaning of grief through the five stages of loss* (pp. xi–xv). Simon & Schuster.

Shulman, L. M. (2018). *Before and after loss: A neurologist's perspective on loss, grief, and our brain*. Johns Hopkins University Press.

Van der Kolk, B. (2014). *The body keeps the score*. Penguin Books.

Weller, F. (2015). *The wild edge of sorrow: Rituals of renewal and the sacred work of grief*. North Atlantic Books.

Wolfelt, A. (2006). *Companioning the bereaved: A soulful guide for caregivers*. Companion Press.

Wolfelt, A. (2014). *The depression of grief: Coping with your sadness and knowing when to get help*. Companion Press.

Chapter 2

GRIEF THROUGH THE EYES OF THE MOURNER

A Personal Exploration of the Dark Night of Grief

While I was mourning, the first book that literally fell into my hands off of my father's bookshelf was C.S. Lewis's (1961) *A Grief Observed*. Here, one of my dad's favorite authors narrates his experiences with grief after the sudden passing of his wife. Not only did his words describe my own emotional upheaval with grief to a T, but the first-person narrative writing style connected directly to my bereavement on a much deeper level. It was as though his words jumped out of the page and landed directly into the core of my pain, simultaneously providing me with some sort of relief. I realized that when honoring one's journey through loss, the author's words must reach deep into those liminal spaces, soothing the wounds of those who cannot.

In honor of C.S. Lewis's brilliant rendition of his brave attempt to reconcile with loss, I, too, attempt to authentically weave my narratives of grief throughout this chapter which explores grief literature through the eyes of the mourner. The central points drawn out of scientific research are aligned with my reactions and responses to grief. As Muller (1993) suggests,

> Our own wounds can be vehicles for exploring our essential nature, revealing the deepest textures of our heart and soul, if only we will sit with them, open ourselves to the pain, and allow ourselves to be taught, without holding back, without blame. (p. 8)

Thus, by reviewing our current understanding of grief, I explore the seams of my wounds, opening them again and taking a look at the pain caused by the experience of loss through death. Then only can the true impact of grief be felt and understood deeply—subjectively. Each section throughout the next three chapters begins with an epigraph of well-known authors, adding to the argument that, historically, writing has been an effective tool used to process grief and express the complexity of sorrow following the loss of a loved one.

The Impact of Grief

No one ever told me that grief felt so like fear. I am not afraid, but the sensation is like being afraid. The same fluttering in the stomach, the same restlessness, the yawning. I keep on swallowing....There is a sort of invisible blanket between the world and me.

—C.S. Lewis, *A Grief Observed*

I sat in the empty row of chairs outside my father's hospital room contemplating, for the first time, the severity of the situation: the fragile line between life and death and the impact that grief would have on my family, and me—a quiet, highly sensitive, and empathic human being. I repeatedly pressed my thumbs into the palms of my hands to make sure I was present with my thoughts, to make sure I was still alive. From time to time, I shifted to turning, twisting, and adjusting my father's rings, now placed on my fingers. The doctors had asked me to remove his jewelry, the same way I had been asked to remove my grandfather's jewelry in a hospital in India 20 years prior. The symbolism of the never-ending cycle in a family's lineage was evident, and the passing of the torch from one generation to the next had already begun. I flashed back to 12 years prior, when I sat in the same hospital, overlooking the Glenmore Reservoir, contemplating the next steps after my father's quadruple bypass open-heart surgery. But this transition was different. This time my spirit was not preparing for life after a heart attack; it was preparing for life after death. And perhaps, because my 19-year-old self did not cope well with tragic circumstances, I had consciously decided at 31 to face grief head-on with both my heart and eyes wide open. In the whole span of my life, this moment was my most courageous. Adarkar and Keiser (2007) posit that "when we are mindful of such emotions, we not only learn more about our own mental landscape, but we also see how we are capable of these emotions and how we can harness them" (p. 258). As I entered life after loss, I had to decide how to heal the magnanimous hole left by my father's death. The choice was mine. But, as with all human endeavors, I knew an unwavering level of effort and commitment would produce better results. And here, I decided I was all in.

Defining Grief

I understood then that when you miss a thing it leaves a hole that only the thing you miss can fill.

—Richard Wagamese, *Indian Horse*

Grief results from any situation where a significant loss has occurred, such as through death or non-death losses like divorce, health, identity, property, employment, financial, social, cultural, spiritual, or transgenerational trauma. Attig (1991) explains that grief, "as an emotion is a complex experience consisting of the well-founded belief that a major loss has occurred, the desire that it not have occurred, and the feelings of pain and anguish over the impossibility of fulfilling that desire" (p. 388). Although grief is a normal, natural reaction to the loss of any kind, this book explores the impact of bereavement caused by loss through the circumstance of death. The technical definition of *grief* is pertinent and regarded as "the psychobiological response to bereavement whose hallmark is a blend of yearning and sadness, along with thoughts, memories, and images of the deceased person" (Shear, 2012, p. 120). However, the wording of Merriam-Webster's (2021) online dictionary definition, presented in Chapter 1, more accurately aligned with my encounter. Since grief is unlike any other emotion due to its ability to evoke deep, poignant distress with no solution in sight, the definition we use to describe the phenomenon should be as close to this feeling as possible—the words must reach the core of the pain.

Death is a universal occurrence—however, grief, contrary to popular belief, is not. Grief is a complex, unique, and subjective journey that appears in its own time after a loved one has died (Bonanno, 2009; Doka, 2016). A person can experience many different types of grief, some being absent, acute, anticipatory, ambiguous, collective, cumulative, delayed, disenfranchised, and normal (or uncomplicated) grief (Parkes & Prigerson, 2010; Shear, 2015; Worden, 2018). Normal grief is a common reaction to death, whereas a person's response is initially intense, but subsides within a reasonable length of time, usually around the six-month mark. The grief I experienced was unusually acute, lasting beyond the socially acceptable timeframe, and the symptoms continued to escalate rather than abate (Shear, 2015). This form of mourning, referred to as prolonged, complicated, or traumatic grief, occurs in roughly 7% of the bereaved population (Shear, 2012). Moreover, according to the *International Classification of Diseases* (ICD-11), prolonged grief disorder is:

> A persistent and pervasive grief response characterized by longing or persistent preoccupation with the deceased, accompanied by intense emotional pain (e.g., sadness, guilt, anger, denial, blame, difficulty accepting the death, feeling one has lost part of one's self, an inability to have a positive mood, emotional numbness, or difficulty in engaging with social or other activities). A grief response that has persisted for an abnormally long period of time after the loss, clearly exceeding expected social, cultural, or religious norms. (Shear, 2015, p. 155)

These symptoms stayed active for the first three years of my mourning. And, when assessing myself on Boelen and Smid's (2017) Traumatic Grief Inventory Self-Report version (TGI-SR), I fell under the 'always' category for all 18 symptoms, persistently, for the first two years. My father did not have a violent death—*it was the opposite*—but his death was untimely, unexpected, and to some extent perceived as preventable due to the lack of a proper diagnosis. He was also my primary parent since infancy and the person I was most attached to throughout my life. According to Rando (1993), all of these reasons can accumulate and contribute to complicated mourning. Although I would eventually come to understand that separation distress, and not necessarily traumatic distress, was the basis of my complicated grief (Parkes & Prigerson, 2010), I had already begun examining my reactions and responses to his death using intentionality: "When the mind becomes conscious of something, when it 'knows' something, it reaches out to, and into, that object" (Crotty, 1998, p. 44). As time went on, I became somewhat infatuated with understanding why I had such an acute reaction to the loss of my father. I had expected to be devastatingly sad, but I had not accounted for all expressions of grief, such as the severe impairment of my day-to-day living. Some members of the grieving community may show little or no outward signs of experiencing grief at all, while others are unable to hide their agony. Throughout my bereavement, I belonged to the latter group.

The Experience of Grief

If all else perished, and he remained, I should still continue to be; and if all else remained, and he were annihilated, the universe would turn to a mighty stranger.

—Emily Brontë, *Wuthering Heights*

Simply put, my experiences with grief were catastrophic. If I were to combine my life's worth of challenges, still, they would not hold a candle to the pain I felt after losing my father. Wolfelt (2003) emphasizes that "the stronger your attachment to the person who died, the more difficult your grief journey will be…the more torn apart you will feel after the death" (p. 36). I expected the forcefulness of my grief; ever since I can remember, I was overly attached to my dad. Yet, as my suffering grew and the likelihood of my grief weakening over time diminished, I began to contemplate the true nature and depth of my relationship with my father. Eventually, while preparing my thesis, my doctoral supervisor, Dr. Ian Winchester, asked me a pivotal question, *If you had lost your mother instead, would you still be pursuing this work?* After a short pause, I replied no. *But why not?* The love I have for both parents is genuine and distributed equally, albeit in different ways. So then, *what is the crucial difference between the two most important relationships in my life?* Bowlby (1998) reveals, "in understanding an individual's response to a loss it is necessary to take into account not only the structure of that individual's personality but also the patterns of interaction in which [s]he was engaging with the person now lost" (p. 212).

In search of a more explicit answer, I examined different layers of our relationship, carefully scanning the qualities, distinctions, genetics, and personality traits that composed our father–daughter dynamic. By engaging in this deliberate cognitive process, slowly, the reason became clear: *I am a replica of my father.* In other words, my identity revolved around his. In their book, *A General Theory of Love*, Lewis et al. (2001) explore that "the stability of an individual mind—what we

know as *identity*—exists only because some neural pathways endure…
it lies at the heart of who we are and who we can become" (p. 100).
From the time I was a baby and placed in my father's arms, I believe
that my neural pathways attached and reinforced themselves around
him, my primary caregiver. And from that time onward, whatever action I took in life looked for his response to guide my direction. Thus,
when my father died, my identity shattered, and disarray took its place.
Doidge (2007) explains that,

> We grieve by calling up one memory at a time, reliving it, and then letting it
> go. At a brain level we are turning on each of the neural networks that were
> wired together to form our perception of the person, experiencing the memo-
> ry with exceptional vividness, then saying good-bye one network at a time. In
> grief, we *learn* to live without the one we love, but the reason this lesson is so
> hard is that we first must *unlearn* the idea that the person exists and can still
> be relied on. (p. 118)

Unlearning to live in a world without my father erupted my neural
networks into chaos and left my mind in a zone of unmitigated disaster. To work through my internal and existential crisis, I had to relearn
the world around me and continue to find meaning in my suffering
through past, present, and future narratives (Attig, 2011).

My father was not only my caregiver growing up but, for most of
my life, I was also a caregiver for my father, paying meticulous attention to his medical, emotional, and dietary needs. And, as his illness
escalated in the hospital, so did my level of care and attentiveness. After he died, I experienced the severe aftermath of no longer being *my
father's keeper*. Caregiver withdrawal became a heart-wrenching reper-
cussion of losing him, which again took a toll on my identity. At the
core of my being, I no longer knew who I was without him. Bonanno
(2009) contributes to this notion, stating,

> People suffering from prolonged grief…feel as if *everything* is missing. With
> prolonged grief, the loss of identity is profound. Whatever life was about
> before the loss no longer seems to matter. Whatever goals or interests the
> bereaved survivor had, whatever were his or her [or their] sources of pleasure,
> are simply no longer important. In the simplest terms, he or she [or they] has
> [have] lost the focus in life. (p. 97)

I had to shift my sense of self, transferring decision-making processes
that relied on my father to me. I went through a change that Neimeyer

(2001) refers to as "deep revisions in…her self-definition" (loc. 181) to develop a greater understanding of who I now was in the world.

From a young age, I had faced traumatic experiences that caused me to stop and analyze my specific emotional responses as they arose. Because of this, I consider myself to be a highly resilient person. However, this did not automatically contribute to my resiliency in grieving. Inexplicable symptoms and surprising physical reactions to my father's death emerged, inhibiting me from fully interacting with my surroundings. Grief was the rare occasion that forced me to stop and sit with my whole being. I was no longer merely experiencing an identity crisis but a multilayered and multidimensional one as well. And due to the complex nature of my grief and the numerous health complications that surfaced, I went in search of answers that could ease my disturbances. Rando (1993) confirms that,

> Grief is experienced in four major ways: psychologically (through affects, cognitions, perceptions, attitudes, and philosophy/spirituality), behaviourally (through personal action, conduct, or demeanor), socially (through reactions to and interactions with others), and physically (through bodily symptoms and physical health). (p. 22)

To understand my encounter with grief, I had to understand the parts of the whole individually: the physical, the social, the psychological, the behavioral, and the spiritual. Next, I had to acknowledge how my father was embedded into each section of my being, ensuring my life ran smoothly like a well-oiled machine. Then, I had to comprehend that the oil ran dry, and that no matter how much I pretended to be okay, I was unable to operate. Last, I had to dig deep into my spiritual reserve to muster up the fortitude required to permit healing, establish continuing ties with him in a new form, and allow the spokes of my life to slowly begin turning once more.

The Physical Responses to Grief

I tightened my grip on my father's hand. The old, familiar fear: not to lose him…

After my father's death, nothing could touch me anymore.

—Elie Wiesel, *Night*

The physical responses to grief are vast, including, but not limited to the following: increased weight, decreased weight, an overflow of memories, memory loss, insomnia, oversleeping, exhaustion, alertness, unawareness, numbness, oversensitivity, increased heart rate, shallow breathing, abdominal pains, nausea, tightness in the chest and throat, panic, and weakness of the body (Doka, 2016; Worden, 2018). Realistically, the physical symptoms of grief are an endless list of oxymorons that not only accompany intense emotional waves but frequently amplify them. For instance, even though I had lost a significant amount of weight post-loss, my body remained deadweight, restricting my movement and increasing my frustration. And since I could not control my physical responses to grief, I realized that my attachment to my father began at the cellular level. Lewis et al. (2001) elaborate on the difference between short-term and prolonged separation: "Prolonged separation affects more than feelings. A number of somatic parameters go haywire in despair. Because separation deranges the body, losing relationships can cause physical illness" (p. 76). Not only did my grief materialize physical illness, but it also interfered with the functioning of all five of my physical senses.

Taste. Physically, my appetite was the first sense to diminish. My desire to eat decreased during the stage of anticipatory grief while my father was in the hospital, and slowly, I formed an aversion to food altogether. It would be considered a good day if either of us had even one meal. Yet, morning, noon, and night, black coffee was the only thing I seemed to be able to consume. *Why black coffee?* It was my father's preferred beverage. *Why couldn't I keep solid food down?* Probably because I was the last one to feed my father, and immediately after, he vomited the entire meal. And as his ability to consume food deteriorated, so did mine. My desire to eat and enjoy food eventually returned—after the first year of performing Indian mourning rituals for his death were completed.

Sound. The craving to hear my father's voice once more, and the ability to still hear him clearly in my mind, left me both satisfied and unfulfilled. I lived in that *liminal* space, a transitory place where my father *exists* and *existed* at the same time. The background noises of the hospital—the whirring sounds of the ventilator, the beeping of the heart monitor, and the incessant ticking of the clock—those noises stayed with me long after we left. But the sounds that haunted me were different; the tones that materialized out of thin air were the ones directly related to my father's condition. The wheeze of my father's extubation liberating him from the ventilator, but marking the beginning of the end; the slight panic in the nurse's voice who rushed into the room because "it's time"; the puff of a final, fading breath that could not find a full exhale; and the crack of my own voice, trembling the first time I had to deliver the news that *he died*. Those sounds remained. Those are the sounds that can be recalled in an instant. And those are the sounds that never vanish nor leave my side.

Smell. Our loved ones have a distinct smell, reminding us of comfort and safety. Panic emerges when the scent of the deceased fades quickly, and the lingering sense of a beloved slowly begins to dull and dwindle. Shear (2015) describes this panic as the "urge to hold onto the deceased person by constantly reminiscing or by viewing, touching, or smelling the deceased person's belongings" (p. 154–155). Wearing my father's clothing calmed me, but washing these items aligned with a form of betrayal, triggering my grief. Dad consistently wore the same shawl every evening while at home, and I was unable to bring myself to wash this shawl for the first two years of my bereavement. I was afraid that I would be washing away the last remnants of him—that once the cloth was immersed in water, the last of his scent would be gone. When I finally accepted that his scent had long since faded on its own, then only did I comprehend that the matter was out of my hands.

At times, the scent of a loved one can unexpectedly surface. Suddenly, in the middle of nowhere, *he is here*. LaGrand (2001) reports that,

> Odors associated with the loved one may range from the perfume or after-shave lotion used to flowers or smoking tobacco. They normally appear to be present at times when there is no available source to account for the odor being experienced. (p. 9)

For me, these odors came in the form of the scent of jasmine flowers, flowers that were native to my father's hometown. Or with the strong scent of church incense that would surface in the hallways of my school. Later, my mother explained to me that traditionally, in our culture, these scents represented visitations from the deceased. Yet, whether these odors were created in my mind or accompanied a deeper spiritual understanding of death did not seem to matter. In my time of need, they brought me comfort and, for a moment, relief.

Sight. The longest I had gone without seeing my father was one month when he traveled to India to take care of his ailing mother. As thoughts of never seeing him again flooded me, I began studying his facial features. I would stare at him closely for long periods while he slept soundly in a hospital bed, attempting to imprint his exact visage in my mind so that, unlike his physical body, the image of him would not have the option of leaving. After he died, my eyes cried in desperation. I had never felt them physically so distraught with fear before. They continuously shifted from side to side, preventing me from adjusting to other sights or reading words on a page. I could *feel* *them* frantically searching for him. And this searching persisted long after his death. When my eyes could no longer find his physical body, they punished me through aches of pain and discomfort. This is what loss did to me; like him, different parts and functions of my body separated from me. I was no longer working as a whole unit; I became internally and externally disjointed. Watching my father die drained all life out of my eyes; everything looked different to me, and I looked permanently different to everyone else. And this altered eyesight was irreversible.

For some grievers, it becomes possible to see the deceased after the death has occurred. Parkes and Prigerson (2010) reassure that "although these phenomena meet the definition of illusions...they are certainly not symptoms of psychosis and simply reflect a strong attachment to the person who died" (p. 71). The morning after my father died, I had an encounter with him. The events of his death had overtaken my thoughts as I tried to make sense of what had happened. All of a sudden, I was snapped out of reality when out of thin air, I caught "fleeting glimpses of the person across the room" (Wolfelt, 2003, p. 52). My father appeared alive and well. Casually, he walked around the corner and into the kitchen, his eyes fixed on mine. "Seeing the deceased loved one in whole or in part is one of the more dramatic and convincing experiences for the mourner" (LaGrand, 2001, p. 6). I stood up in disbelief and cried aloud to those in the room, *Dad! He's here! I see him!* However, just as soon as I saw him, he disappeared just as quickly. The room fell silent as I noticed the quiet, pitiful stares looking back at me. The words choked my speech as I sat back down, exploding into tears, *I know I saw him. He was right here.* The truth of the matter was that I had become a statistic of the bereaved who claim to see or hear their deceased loved one shortly after their demise, and "that 'searching' and 'finding' go together is not surprising" (Parkes & Prigerson, 2010, p. 70).

Because of the persistent suffering felt by my eyes, the only thing I could do to appease this sense was to place photos of my father in every corner of my life, specifically in areas where he spent most of his time. Thus, whether a person is in my home or office, my phone or wallet, they will see a picture of my dad. By choosing to drown out the voices that tried to influence my grief in negative ways—*maybe you shouldn't have so many photos around*—I effectively reduced the fear felt by my sense of sight. Still, I actively use images of my father to provide relief and inspire me to keep moving toward reconciling with his loss.

Touch. Losing the physical touch of my father has been the most challenging sensory experience I have had to come to terms with because this part of loss offers no remedy or solace. As a highly sensitive person (HSP), my body was accustomed to specific tools and strategies that were put in place to protect my nervous system from overstimulation (Aron, 1998), and my father's physical presence was my main source of comfort. Due to financial constraints in my childhood, the four of us lived in a small apartment, and since my brother was older and required his own space, I grew up sleeping in between my parents. And because my mother was often at work, my periods of rest were synchronous with lying beside my father: "The mammalian nervous system depends for its neurophysiologic stability on a system of interactive coordination, wherein steadiness comes from synchronization with nearby attachment figures" (Lewis et al., 2001, p. 84). Thus, even as an adult, if I walked into the room and Dad was sleeping, I would nap beside him and fall into a deep sleep, waking up feeling refreshed and reenergized.

My father was a severe diabetic who took insulin daily and required a medicated lotion to soften the effects of diabetic dermopathy. Since I was a child, I carried out both tasks religiously as a medical and cultural obligation. As his final days approached in the hospital, nightly, we would sit with his legs on my lap as I applied this lotion for hours, watching him drift in and out of consciousness. My hands were numb to the pain, insisting on squeezing his skin, knowing that soon it would not be so readily available. *What purpose will these hands have after he's gone?* Often, I reminisced on the importance of his touch in reference to my life. I remembered how in my most harrowing moments when encountering the ills of the world, my father's physical presence was the only cure. We were always together, holding hands and thriving from the connection that only the human touch can bring. *Who will protect me once this armor is gone?* The only object standing in between me and real suffering was his body.

Even though we knew we had a reciprocal relationship of easing each other's pain, it became more evident to others when he fell ill, and his visitors observed our ability in action and pointed it out. They noted how my touch visibly reduced my father's distress or allowed us to continue communicating with one another while he was on life support and no longer verbal. Lewis et al. (2001) elaborate on our looped system,

> Because human physiology is (at least in part) an open-loop arrangement, an individual does not direct all of his own functions. A second person transmits regulatory information that can alter hormone levels, cardiovascular function, sleep rhythms, immune function, and more—inside the body of the first. The reciprocal process occurs simultaneously: the first person regulates the physiology of the second, even as he himself is regulated. Neither is a functioning whole on his own; each has open loops that only somebody else can complete. Together they create a stable, properly balanced pair of organisms. And the two trade their complementary data through the open channel their limbic connection provides. (p. 85)

This is a perfect summary of our father–daughter dynamic. As important and necessary as our verbal communication, our non-verbal communication was likewise essential for our survival.

In most North American cultures, mourners are often encouraged to remove the deceased's belongings. The person's possessions are not revered for what they are, an indispensable aspect of touch. And when visitors entered our home, this was also the case: *Don't you think you should put those away? You will never move forward with all of his things out in the open like this.* However, we were not fooled by false notions. We knew that the griever must do what feels right for them—that we had a choice in the matter. Attig (1991) reinforces a grieving family's prerogative, stating, "they can choose to keep, discard, or postpone until later decisions about what is to be done with physical effects, pictures, mementos, and other objects that have significant relation to the deceased" (p. 391). Objects hold meaning for us, which is why we link them to our living milestones. Now, we must learn to link them in death also. Thus, when his physical body began slipping through my fingers, I placed his jewelry on them; when they unwrapped his body of his clothes, I swaddled myself in them; when his items lost their owner, I gave them a new home. These *linking objects* were pertinent to my healing (Rando, 1993; Wolfelt, 2003). I intended to envelop myself in my father's touch as much as I possibly could—and so, if the items touched him, they needed to touch me too.

Later on, while reading *A General Theory on Love*, I understood that losing physical contact with my parent was responsible for the physiological changes that ensued. Here, the authors presented Dr. Hofer's observations on the chaos that occurs when removing a mother rat from her pups: "Once separated from their attachment figures, mammals spiral down into a somatic disarray that can be measured from the outside and painfully felt on the inside" (Lewis et al., 2001, p. 83). Hofer discovered that human-made conditions were unsuccessful at reducing these effects, yet fragmented items that held the mother's sensory qualities could restore one physiologic aspect at a time. It seems as though I had come to this understanding on my own. Mimicking my father's touch with his belongings was not just an intuitive measure but an unshakeable understanding that the sensory feel of his linking objects was capable of regulating the physiological mayhem that accompanied the loss of my primary parent.

The Social Responses to Grief

I felt very still and empty, the way the eye of a tornado must feel, moving dully along in the middle of the surrounding hullabaloo.

—Sylvia Plath, *The Bell Jar*

Reintegrating myself into my surrounding society post-loss was an arduous task, and perhaps one that I failed miserably at: "Trauma can turn the whole world into a gathering of aliens…many traumatized people find themselves chronically out of sync with the people around them" (Van der Kolk, 2014, p. 81). And I stood out like a sore thumb.

Quickly, I understood that "loss disrupts our story" (Attig, 2011, p. xlvii), and my story had split into two versions—the girl who had a father and the girl who did not. Yet, the world kept turning, and the people around me kept moving and talking and smiling and laughing and living. It was I who could no longer find substantial reasons to continue to do any of those things.

The social responses to grief traveled along a narrow spectrum of people who were either fully supportive and attentive to my mourning needs or detached and unfazed by my loss. Dr. Alan Wolfelt (2003), a grief specialist, describes this spectrum as the "Rule of Thirds": when a person endures the loss of a loved one, one-third of the people will be truly helpful and supportive, one third will remain neutral to grief, and one third will be judgmental and harmful toward the reconciliation process (p. 127–128). Unfortunately, in my case, once the funeral passed, most of my social support fell away. Many vanished from my life because they *didn't know what to say*, while others relied on an imaginary other, excusing their absence by assuming I was already overflowing with support. At first, I was shocked by the lack of empathy. Their actions led to disbelief, anger, and bitterness that they even had the luxury of opting out, which, in turn, exacerbated my grief. Eventually, my anger turned to contemplation, my bitterness turned to compromise, and my disbelief turned to curiosity: *Why is it that they don't know what to say?* Culturally, something was amiss. I concluded that perhaps, due to my age group (then, early thirties), many of my friends had yet to experience a primary loss and could be deemed grief-illiterate.

Grief illiteracy condones the use of clichés, platitudes, and insensitive remarks: *he's in a better place now, be happy; at least he lived a good life, be appreciative; at least you had him for this long, be thankful; at least you had a father, be grateful.* They demonstrate not knowing that grief, in its essence, is an overflow of the gratitude you carry for your loved one. Moreover, the automatic response to witnessing natural emotion—*you have to stay strong*—is used to deflect the complicated layers of grief and should be eliminated from our interactions altogether. Upon hearing this repeated effort from others, I often wondered what their definition of strength was: *is it to passively and submissively endure the complexities of life?* No. Authentic strength derives from actively engaging with the emotional landscape of the human condition; first, succumbing to, and then, rising out of one's suffering—not maneuvering around it.

Such illiteracy, not having the language to engage with death and grief, materializes into inaccurate perceptions of grieving, false societal expectations, and unrealistic timelines for reconciliation with loss (Devine, 2017; Doka, 2016). *It's been four months. How long do you think this will take?* Obtuse statements cause the griever to doubt their ability to heal, negatively influencing their unique journey through grief. Some feel ashamed for not meeting these expectations, while others become mute on the subject altogether. Alongside these responses, I became increasingly frustrated and disappointed with myself for not being able to grieve fast enough. And, every so often, a narcissistic quality arose in others, whereas my father's death became about their *alive* and *well* family members. They tried to relate to my grief using unrelatable terms. Consequently, instead of receiving comfort, I found myself comforting or consoling others because of the loss of my father as they contemplated the *possible* loss of theirs. Or, I would have to minimize my grief because a much worst-case scenario existed somewhere out there: *At least losing a father follows the natural order of life.* Suddenly, two groups of people emerged—those who had experienced a life-changing loss and those who had not.

Van der Kolk (2014) supports that "after trauma the world becomes sharply divided between those who know and those who don't. People who have not shared the traumatic experience cannot be trusted, because they can't understand it" (p. 18). Sigmund Freud himself found fault in his theories, as written before the loss of his daughter; the experience of her loss changed his perception and understanding of grief (Klass & Steffen, 2018). Within a short span, I awoke to the fact that the path to reconciliation would be a lot longer and lonelier than I expected, and they convinced me that: *Grieving is something you have to do on your own.*

As a result of my paralyzing grief and its inability to recede, I physically withdrew from my social circles and isolated myself, creating distance from the misdirection and judgment of others. For the first year of my bereavement, I stayed hidden in my apartment. Darkness surrounded me, and so, I surrendered and cocooned. My highly sensitive nature needed silence to heal, and I could no longer bear the mounting pressure placed on me to be normal again. I was exhausted by dead-end advice that led me further away from fully grieving the loss of my father, and I was tired of hearing that my grief was unhealthy. Grief was overpowering me—not the other way around. Attig (1991) supports that,

> Grieving is a process of recovery that at best brings the bereaved back to their original healthy state. They have no more control over the pace or nature of the recovery than those with physical illnesses have conscious influence over the processes of physical recovery. (p. 387)

But, as with all invisible struggles, empathy was limited and selective. Some even dared to tell me that feeling my pain is not what my father would have wanted. *How do you know what he would want for me?* He raised me to face my pain courageously, with persistence and fortitude. And that's exactly what I was going to do.

Last, and perhaps the most devastating social consequence of my prolonged grief, was that I was forced to become cognizant of my social circles, specifically, the brittle relationships I had forged and sustained for too long. Some of my most intimate friendships easily disbanded after proving to be apathetic to my mourning needs. "It's one of the cruelest aspects of intense loss: at a time when you most need love and support, some friends either behave horribly or they disappear altogether" (Devine, 2017, p. 81). These secondary losses were unexpected, *eye-opening*, cutting ties with those less compassionate who proved harmful to my grieving process. Their actions ranged anywhere from not visiting my father in the hospital over the two months he was admitted, to listening to poor excuses as to why someone could not attend his funeral, to more serious offenses, such as acting disrespectfully during our Indian cultural practice of solemn observance after a loved one's death, shattering my understanding of community: "In the interval, there are prohibitions on weddings [and celebrations], pilgrimages, the completion of new houses, sexual intercourse, and the preparation of certain foods [and alcohol consumption]" (Mosse, 1996, p. 465). Until this point in my life, I had given a lot of my love and attention to the people around me, pouring my heart and soul out freely, expecting little in return. Yet, the one time I needed authentic reciprocity, it turned out I would not be given the same consideration. And this broke me, altering the core of my caring nature and enforcing a newfound state of hypervigilance. Van der Kolk (2014) attests to this need, stating,

> Social support is not the same as merely being in the presence of others. The critical issue is *reciprocity*: being truly heard and seen by the people around us, feeling that we are held in someone else's mind and heart. (p. 81)

Out of all the disasters one can face, grief seems to be the occasion that naturally causes us to expect more from the people around us. And lacking this reciprocal support, a witnessing of my suffering—my grief took notice, cleansing those who no longer fit the transformed version of me that was born from loss.

Luckily, new and unexpected support sprang into action, usually from other members of the grieving community or those who did remember the shoulder they leaned on in their time of need. As Tedeschi and Calhoun (2006) comment, "some bereaved persons are fortunate to have, or to find, people who will engage in supportive responses and considerations over the extensive period of time that bereaved people may need to consider spiritual matters" (p. 110). Being the sole proprietor of my own Reiki healing practice, many of my clients reached out to me; some even attended the funeral, or visited me in the months after he died: *You helped me through the darkest time in my life, now I want to be there for yours.* My colleagues at the school where I taught, specifically those who knew what loss entailed, kept a close eye on me, ensuring that I was being cared for both inside and outside the workplace. And, I had two trustworthy, faithful friends who picked up my shattered pieces and held onto them *until I was ready* to glue myself back together. Lastly, I formed new friendships by seeking out grief support groups. It was easier to be around people who understood the pain and unpredictable path of grief, those who would allow me to sit and feel through the agony. By forming stronger ties within the community and learning how to companion grief myself, I understood the value of bringing this skill set into schools to instill these essential soft skills in students. Therefore, feeling confident in one's socially sensitive response to death and grief can be a viable outcome of grief education.

The Psychological Responses to Grief

I am unable to come to You

Or from core of heart invoke

The pang of separation pains me so

My heart does burn and choke.

—Kabīr, *Kabir Dohe, Couplet 201* (translated by G.N. Das)

Over the final fifty-four days of my father's life, my mind festered with trauma, witnessing his slow deterioration. The mental distress I endured eventually manifested as the psychological responses to grief. First, my body mimicked my father's symptoms as they appeared throughout his illness. Doka (2016) reveals how "some people experience physical symptoms similar to those suffered by the person who died. Sometimes the reactions have a strong symbolic connection to the loss, such as heartache" (p. 27). In my case, this was exactly true. When my father's body began preparing for death, I observed his excessive sweating for three days. The sweating was so intense that no matter how many times I attempted to dry him, the towel remained drenched. I could not prevent it, contain it, or stop it—my heart panicked with denial. After the funeral was over, my body mirrored the experience. For three days exactly, I was bedridden, profusely sweating out my visions of him. I realize now that my body was imitating more than meets the eye. Perhaps, I, too, was preparing for a new life, perspiring out my denial at the same time.

Next, when I overheard the doctor state that my father *had a series of mini heart attacks over the course of the night,* I was then bombarded with, and forced to concede to, a year full of chest pains. I had read that separation pain, chest pain, and tightness in the chest and throat were common responses to grief. *But this can't only be grief, can it?* Debilitated by the pain, I began sweeping the Internet for a better answer and concluded that maybe I suffered from broken heart syndrome, also known as stress-induced cardiomyopathy. According to the American Heart Association (2019), it is "sudden, intense chest pain—the reaction to a surge of stress hormones—that can be caused by an emotionally stressful event" (para 4). *That made more sense.* But still, I was not completely satisfied by this answer. This pain was different, a bolt of lightning striking my arteries, a sensation that could only be created through a tangible, physical ailment. And as the unruly chest pains continued adversely affecting my daily routines, I decided to visit my family doctor. Cardiovascular disease has been noted, especially in women, to increase shortly before or after the death of a loved one (Parkes & Prigerson, 2010). *Dad was a heart patient, after all; maybe my stress has triggered my genetics.* After analyzing the results of the electrocardiogram, the doctor informed me that the thunderous chest pain—as well as all of the other extreme physical symptoms I had experienced since his death—were psychosomatic. *Psychosomatic? I'm creating phantom pain? How is that possible?* Parkes and Prigerson (2010) state that "a group of psychiatrists developed the theory that it is the feelings of helplessness and hopelessness that may accompany loss that are responsible for physical illness" (p. 22). The rationalization within my mind to explain my crippling pain was endless, and perhaps this incessant reasoning itself was to blame.

Finally, as I watched my father take his last breath, simultaneously a short, forceful breath shot out of my lungs. A pang of pain ran through the center of my chest as I felt what could only be explained as my heart breaking down the centerline. For the entire first year of my bereavement, this sharp squeezing remained, accompanied by extreme anxiousness, panic attacks, and unexpected, consistent shortness of breath. In their study of grief in adult life, Parkes and Prigerson (2010) define these episodic pangs as: "an episode of severe anxiety and psychological pain. At such times, lost people are strongly missed and the survivors sob or cry aloud for them" (p. 49). The uncontrollable crying caused my hands to tremor whenever I sat still, and without realizing it, I began tapping my chest to soothe my racing, aching heart. I sat like this for hours, *tapping.* And after the six-month mark had passed, and my symptoms worsened—the choking, the spasming, the searing pain—my acute grief grew complicated, profoundly impairing my ability to function. I tried to avoid or distract my grief, but traumatic scenes from the hospital, "insistent thoughts or images of the deceased" (Shear, 2015, p. 154), forced their way to the front of my mind.

The faintest reminders of my father's death then pushed my body into fight-or-flight: "when something reminds traumatized people of the past, their right brain reacts as if the traumatic event were happening in the present" (Van der Kolk, 2014, p. 45). For two years, these phantom pains remained, and my short, lifeless breaths overtook my ability to hold conversations with other people. At last, it dawned on me that two people died in the room that night—my father and a version of me that no longer existed. In a letter I wrote to my father four months after his demise, I noted: *My world has become so quiet—that, at times, I, myself, don't realize I am in the room.* I became unrecognizable, even to me, and had to relearn how to exist in a world without my primary parent and closest bond (Attig, 2011).

The Behavioral Responses to Grief

The grief hath craz'd my wits.

—William Shakespeare, *King Lear*

Being surrounded by crowds of people at the start of my grieving process created a barrier between me and the disaster waiting to strike. Initially, my behavior displayed somewhat supernatural abilities. Running on minimal sleep and little to eat, I was still able to act as an excellent caregiver at my father's bedside. In these moments, I learned the true meaning of unconditional love. Because of my calm demeanor and reasonable approach to the climactic aspects and downfalls of my father's health, I was labeled as the *strong one*. Visibly, I looked upset, but I was not communicating my fears or expressing much outward emotion. A true introvert, I suppressed the inner chaos that accompanies these life and death situations to ensure I placed my father at the forefront of each day. And once he died, I channeled all of my energy into the closing events of his life. We had to let our extended family know, our friends know, and the priests know. I had to write the eulogy, obituary, and create a slideshow. We had to arrange the funeral, pick out the casket, gravesite, and headstone. I had to choose the pallbearers, the format for the service, and what clothes to wear. We had to choose what clothes he would wear. I had to apply for extended leave, make substitute plans, and write 150 report card comments. *There's no time to think about death; I have too much to do instead.* Truthfully, my strength was not motivated by my acceptance of the circumstances but by my lack of conviction that his demise had happened: "Shock, numbness, and disbelief are nature's way of temporarily protecting you from the full reality of the loss. They help insulate you psychologically until you are more able to tolerate what you don't want to believe" (Wolfelt, 2014, p. 11). Thoughts passed through my mind like water flowing through a narrow tunnel, focusing only on what needed to be done at each twist and turn. And, every so often, an unexpected suspicion would appear. *He hasn't really died, has he?* I applied for my Indian visa, booked my airplane ticket, and traveled halfway across the world to Kerala, India, to perform my father's closing rituals. *No, of course not.* I left and did what needed to be done, firmly holding onto the belief that, *when I get back, he'll be sitting in his chair, waiting for me.*

The rituals concluding my father's death were auspiciously carried out; the crowd of support was gone, and now, *so was my father.* The devastation of loss was about to set in, as "trauma shocks the brain, stuns the mind, and freezes the body" (Levine, 2015, p. xxi). My emotional reaction to grief came as no surprise; I had just lost the most important person in my life. But my behavioral responses completely caught me off guard, and everyone took notice. The—*you are so strong*—comments quickly turned into—*but you were so strong before*—not realizing that my toughness then was accumulated and distributed for the sake of my father. As the actuality of his death attempted to ascend from my heart to my mind, I choked, swept under by a tsunami of grief. I imagined the tide would be high, but I was not expecting to be fully submerged under the water. In a symbolic sense, I was being reborn. I had to relearn basic instinctual survival mechanisms for a new world—one that existed without my protector, causing me major distress.

Attig (2011) describes "relearning the world" as "a multi-dimensional process of learning *how to* live meaningfully again after loss" (p. xxxix). For me, this consisted of learning how to walk out of my house and into social settings without bursting into tears; how to hold meaningful conversations with others for extended periods, without tuning them out; how to focus my attention on menial tasks, without my mind transporting me back to the hospital; how to successfully function as a contributing member of society, without feeling hopeless; and how to integrate a new version of myself into the old version of my surroundings, without expectations of change. Relearning the world did not come easy for me and for most of the mourning process, my behavior consisted of avoiding social situations altogether. And, as far as I could tell, social situations did the same to me: "In a death—and grief—avoidant culture, a grieving person becomes the other to whom social structures cannot, and will not, relate—and that avoidance is truly tragic" (Cacciatore, 2017, p. 49).

The raw wounds left by my father's death burst open at the artificial seams, and I was left to suffer, alone. All too familiar situations ensued with devastating consequences. *Mom, where's Dad? In his room?* No, he's not. *Look at the time, I forgot to call Dad!* No, you didn't. *Dad would love this; I'm going to buy it for him.* No, you won't. *I cooked Dad's favorite meal; I'll bring it over for him.* No, you can't. Piece by piece, the face of grief revealed itself. And as more of these pieces joined together to form a clearer picture of the impact of his death, I crumbled. My behavior shifted from disbelief to intense searching, yearning, and pining for him. Without control, I began subconsciously searching for my father everywhere. My mind was so determined to locate his whereabouts that I regularly drifted in and out of daydreams—daily, my father would walk through my classroom door, and I ran toward him, relieved. Or, when the darkness shackled me, the situation flipped, whereas I imagined scenarios that reunited me with him. My desire to live grew achingly faint.

Parkes and Prigerson (2010) explain that "searching is a restless activity in which one moves towards possible locations of a lost object. The person who is searching has to select places in which to look, move towards them, and scan them" (p. 54). I would go to my father's favorite places and desperately search for his face in the crowd, waiting for him to appear and wake me from this nightmare. When I could not find him in those spaces, I frantically searched through his belongings, drawers, cabinets, briefcases, suitcases, and closets; any area that belonged to him was at my disposal to provide me with clues to where he went. My other family members did not understand this part of my grief; they did not experience the same relentless urge to continue searching for my father. Bonanno (2009) supports their perception that,

> The paradox of yearning brings no comfort, only deeper pain…their loved one is dead and cannot be found. Their search is endless, hopeless, and futile—a bit like chasing a ghost—and it brings only more and more pain. (p. 98)

However, even though my *search* and *rescue* did not make sense to them, it made sense to me: "We contend that the searching behaviour of the bereaved person is not 'aimless' at all. It has the specific aim of finding the one who is gone" (Parkes & Prigerson, 2010, p. 56). And often, my searching would yield comforting results such as finding a prepurchased early birthday card, old pictures, lost jewelry items, or the poem printed at the start of this book. *Dad wanted me to find this, and so I did.*

I resumed work two days after returning from India. Genuinely, I tried to appear healthy and capable of continuing with my day-to-day affairs. *I cannot let my grief affect the students or my ability to teach them.* At the time, I believed this to be the case—that I appeared to be coping, and no one knew otherwise. But as I began writing field notes for my autoethnography, the truth came out. I asked friends, colleagues, and students for their observations of me during my mourning period. Here is how they described me: *very quiet, shaky voice, or mute; here but not here; hollow; zombie-like or zoned-out; shell-like or protected; fatigued or exhausted; dazed and confused; awkward smiling; limited vocabulary; not present and visibly in so much pain;* and, *all-consumed by grief.* I was living out Lewis's (1961) description of grief as feeling "mildly drunk, or concussed. There is a sort of blanket between me and the world. I find it hard to take in what anyone says" (p. 1). When people talked to me, they would have to repeat what they said. And when I spoke to them, they would ask me to repeat myself. I tried as hard as I could to seem normal, but in the end, my efforts were obviously in vain.

Due to previous experiences in my life, I knew that I had once again fallen prey to Post-Traumatic Stress Disorder (PTSD). Van der Kolk (2014) defines PTSD as occurring when,

> A person is exposed to a horrendous event…which results in a variety of manifestations: intrusive re-experiencing of the event (flashbacks, bad dreams, feeling as if the event were occurring), persistent and crippling avoidance (of people, places, thoughts, or feelings associated with trauma, sometimes with amnesia for important parts of it), and increased arousal (insomnia, hypervigilance, or irritability).…The trauma may be over, but it keeps being replayed in continually recycling memories and in a reorganized nervous system. (p. 158–159)

The first six months post-loss was as described here. I would be in the middle of teaching a lesson when suddenly, I could hear the nurse telling me, *it's time*, blocking out all other sounds from the vicinity. Simultaneously, an image of my father taking his last breath would force its way to the front of my mind, causing me to lose sight of the present moment. When I was alone in the evenings, my thoughts were intrusive, permitting only the idea of him dying to pass through my mind. And, when I slept, my dreams replayed a series of harrowing scenes from the hospital: "In sleep and at times of relaxed attention painful memories tend to float back into our mind and sufferers from PTSD find themselves reliving the trauma yet again" (Parkes & Prigerson, 2010, p. 45). Upon waking, I would uncontrollably reach over to the nightstand, questioning, *Did Mom call?* I was carrying out a routine embedded in my system over the last few weeks of his life. And, every night, without fail, I awoke at the exact time of his death, *1:41 a.m.*, a new imprint tattooed on my biological clock. These examples of trauma-induced memories "erupt[ed] involuntarily" (Levine, 2015, p. 8), were "overwhelming, unbelievable, and unbearable" (Van der Kolk, 2014, p. 197), and were based on personal meaning connected directly to my father's death.

During the day, my body was riddled with fear, enraged by psychosomatic pain, and battling emotionally induced breathing difficulties, such as deep intense sighing. Parkes and Prigerson (2010) posit that "irregular sighs are thought to represent inspiratory spasms of crying or sobbing, and the term 'choked with grief' reflects this" (p. 51). I was permanently in a state of hyperarousal; I could feel the adrenaline coursing through my veins. And, since "the stress hormones of traumatized people...take much longer to return to baseline and spike quickly and disproportionately in response to mildly stressful stimuli" (Van der Kolk, 2014, p. 46), I was unable to come down from this response to danger. If any external stimuli triggered a bodily response (for example, a fire drill), I would be right back in the hospital with my father, unable to function in real-time. *It's okay, Ms. Mathew, I'll take attendance.* I could not communicate to others what had happened to my father then, and I was powerless to verbalize what was happening to me now. Because, as Van der Kolk (2014) asserts, "traumatized people have enormous difficulty telling other people what has happened to them...trauma by nature drives us to the edge of comprehension, cutting us off from language based on common experience or an imaginable past" (p. 43). The only option that provided relief was to refrain from leaving my apartment and limit as much social interaction as possible:

> We may control anxiety by shutting ourselves up in a safe place (usually our home), avoiding people and situations that remind us of the trauma, and deliberately filling our minds with thoughts and activities that will distract us from the horror. (Parkes & Prigerson, 2010, p. 45)

Thus, my evenings were spent at home, attempting to avoid external stimulation, wrapped in my father's belongings, and crying out the enormous amount of accumulated grief that begged for release. Although I found these acts beneficial and healing, I walked a fine line. Once the summer months arrived, and I had nothing but his death to occupy my mind, I fell into a deep depression, unable to leave my home until the next school year began.

Lastly, the most prominent and unforeseen behavior was that I suffered from severe memory loss. The capacity or extent to which I could remember things was unreliable and often fragmented. *What was that person's name? Where do my things keep disappearing to? Where am I? What year is it?* For three years after he died, I remained 31. Or, most days, I was stuck in January of 2017. *Ms. Mathew, the date is wrong on the board again.* With his last breath, all sense of time vanished. My mind could not comprehend that the earth continued to turn beyond his death. Shulman (2018) explains that "dissociation is usually triggered by strong emotionally painful stimuli...detachment from reality...when something happens that you can't control—when you feel helpless in the face of events that you perceive as a threat" (p. 55). Helplessness had become my natural state; it festered inside from his loss and seeped out of my pores into my daily life. I was progressing from one day to the next without any cognizance of how I was doing so. I could not perform menial tasks without feeling frustrated, I could not read words on the page and grasp what they meant, I could not remember people's faces or names or recall how I knew them, and I could not remember standard routines without step-by-step instructions. It was the lowest point of my life, and I had no idea how to make sense of anything around me.

> Grief does that. It rearranges your mind. It takes away skill sets you've had since childhood. It makes even the simplest things hard to follow. It makes

once-familiar things feel arbitrary or confusing. It impacts your memory, your ability to communicate, your capacity for interaction. (Devine, 2017, p. 125)

However, my memory was selective, as I could remember some things like: *he came to the hospital to visit dad,* or *she attended the funeral and came to the burial site.* Those details remain vivid in my memory even today. To move past these traumatized behaviors and regain control over my life, I would have to go on a spiritual quest to make sense of my father's death, rigorously contemplating my spiritual understanding of the events to bring meaning back to my life once more.

The Spiritual Responses to Grief

In the middle of our life journey I found myself in a dark wood. I had wandered from the straight path. It isn't easy to talk about it: it was such a thick, wild, and rough forest that when I think of it my fear returns…I can't offer any good explanation for how I entered it.

—Dante, *Inferno, Canto 1*

My spiritual response to grief began before my father's death occurred. A visceral instinct kicked in that sensed life was transitioning before he was even hospitalized. And by paying close attention to my surroundings and my father's deteriorating actions, a discernment grew, signaling danger ahead. *Why is he falling asleep while unlacing his shoes? Why can't he recognize their faces or recall their names?* A sneaking suspicion, otherwise known as my intuition, was in motion. I began consciously practicing and mastering the art of intuition in my early twenties, a term that Burnham (2011) defines as:

A hunch, a gut feeling, an inspiration, or a premonition, precognition, clairvoyance, clairaudience, clairsentience, prescience, second sight – the shiver of "knowing" that pierces the veil of time and peers briefly into the future or at least into what's not happened yet. (p. 6–7)

I define intuition as a heightened awareness or focused attention that leads us to receive or make reasonable predictions in the present moment. And, because I am a deeply intuitive person, I had a strong knowing, a guiding inner voice that told me my father's life was coming to an end—*one month and five days before it happened.* It was a universal truth I had spent most of my life denying. But late one evening, a premonition revealed a transparent message, reminding me of his impermanence. Eventually, his death would regrettably confirm the accuracy of my intuition, simultaneously distancing me from these instincts and causing me to disengage from my sixth sense for months thereafter.

I was born and raised in Canada, but my ancestral roots stem from India, a religiously diverse nation "known for its rich spiritual heritage" and "unique ways of understanding, experiencing, and expressing spirituality" (Inbadas, 2017, p. 338). Passed down from one generation to the next, Indian civilization has strict spiritual philosophies that have been actively sought by examining direct interpretations of divine knowledge embedded within its framework. The Father of the Nation, Mahatma Gandhi, was well-known for deriving inspiration to conquer his struggles through his daily readings of *The Bhagavad Gita*, one of India's most ancient and holy texts (Hawley, 2011). The consensus in India is that "the concept of the human person is based on the understanding that the human soul is from the divine and is the same substance as its divine source…it is an extension of the divine, a gift of God" (Inbadas, 2017, p. 339).

My father always emphasized the importance of being spiritually aware and consistently engaging in *spiritual literacy*, "the ability to read the signs written in the texts of our own experiences" (Brussat & Brussat, 1998, p. 15). After my schoolwork was completed, lessons on religion, faith, and spirituality took place in his classroom. I enjoyed learning about these teachings as we both had a curiosity about theology, divinity, and the ethereal elements of life that are not always visible to the human eye. Our lineage descends from forefathers who were *scholars*, *teachers*, *healers*, and *priests*. Perhaps this is why whenever my life came to a standstill growing up in the western world, I contemplated the meaning behind my suffering using an eastern, spiritual lens. Because of its rooted historical, cultural, and social significance, spirituality plays a vital role in the development and meaning-making aspects of life for Indians. Thus, my spiritual responses to grief shaped my grieving and healing.

After my father's death, I was enveloped by a spiritual concept known as *the dark night of the soul*. In spiritual literature, it is described as a liminal space of the unknown that materializes during times of great crisis and transformation, symbolically equivalent to the meta-morphosis of a butterfly (LaGrand, 2001; Moore, 2004). At the soul level, life after loss was cocooned in darkness, seeming dismal and bleak. I entered an interval in time where an old self had fallen away, but a new self had not yet made itself known. Often, I wondered if I even wanted to emerge anew; I clung to the darkness because I was uncertain if I could bring my father into the light with me. I was unaware, then, that this is where he would be felt the strongest—in the light. Yet, no matter how hard I tried to push through the thick skin of grief, my spiritual strength continued to plummet. Attig (2011) writes that,

> Profound change in the world calls for profound change in us. But our ego, soul, and spirit are all in crisis. Our disillusioned ego is helpless before the events it could not, and mysteries it cannot, control. Our soul is uprooted and wrenched out of the familiar, doubting if it can ever care so deeply or feel at home again. And our spirit is fearful and discouraged, doubting if it can overcome sorrow, face unwelcome change, or ever know meaning, love, or joy again. (p. xlix)

The spiritual pandemonium that transpired from my father's death created physical unresponsiveness and dread. At times, I had no idea *who* I was, *where* I was, or *what* I was doing. Or, as Bowlby (1961) explains, I experienced a "disorganization of personality accompanied by pain and despair" (p. 319). An enlarged space in my heart reserved for my father was now vacant, and I had no desire to change it or fill it: "We sense that our losses are irretrievable, that we can no longer find meaning, realize value, or know love now that the one we love is dead and cannot return to us" (Attig, 2011, p. xlvii). Not only did my soul lose its soulmate, but as a woman who thrived from finding meaning in her life, everything now seemed meaningless. Bowlby (1961) interprets this as, "interaction between [herself] and [her] world has ceased, not only does [she] experience the world as poor and empty but [she] feels [herself] to be the same" (p. 335). Accordingly, my desire for insignificant things vanished, including food, objects, pleasure, social interactions, and forming close and intimate bonds with other people. My spiritual responses to grief led me to a place of alienation, isolation, desolation, and numbness.

Although I would not physically put myself in harm's way, it felt as though valid reasons to continue developing my story were nonexistent. A life without my father was no life at all, and so I disengaged. As Attig (2019) reasons, "you dwell in a dark place in your heart where missing your loved one consumes you" (p. 30). My physical body was unable to find grounding, and instead, partook in some sort of out-of-body experience where I could no longer feel the natural rhythms of life that were still in motion around me. The psychologist who attended to my grief asked me to put these feelings into words. Having contemplated this a lot already, I swiftly responded, *it feels as though my physical body is here, but my soul is floating above, frantically searching for my father still*. Perhaps this is why Attig (2011) refers to the term *soul* as the "home-seeking aspect of our self that is the driving force within us — that seeks nurture, connection, and grounding in the familiar" (p. xlviii). Passing through the notions of an existential crisis, I began questioning my reality: *Maybe, I am the one who died, and this is my punishment, a life without my father*. At the core of my grief, a sensation emerged of not feeling whole or real, and my surroundings mimicked the same. Parkes and Prigerson (2010) explain that "depersonalization occurs when bereaved people feel as if they are themselves unreal, derealization implies that it is the world that seems unreal. Either or both of these phenomena can occur following bereavement" (p. 77). My potent grief was powerful enough to manifest both depersonalization and derealization, and these extreme responses to loss conveyed I was in a spiritual crisis. Yet, oddly enough, it was this space of confusion that enabled me to go on a spiritual pilgrimage, seeking restitution:

> In that darkness you see things you couldn't see in the daylight. Skills and powers of soul emerge from your frustration and ignorance. The seeds of spiritual faith, perhaps your only recourse but certainly a valuable power, are found in your darkness. The other half of who you are comes into view, and through the dark night you are completed. (Moore, 2004, p. 315)

The path to reconciliation led me to turn inward and listen to my spirit, the "meaning-seeking aspect of our self…[that] strives to overcome adversity, and reaches for transcendent understanding" (Attig, 2011, p. xlvii). I knew that if I were to continue living meaningfully, I would need to find meaning in losing my father; I would need to transform into a better version of myself. In keeping with my Indian cultural traditions, I began asking bigger questions and striving for deeper, spiritual answers, as "Indian philosophy engages with the metaphysical questions arising from the experiences of life where the divine and human share in the formation of understanding" (Inbadas, 2017, p. 339). However, unlike C.S. Lewis's (1961) famous questioning of God's role in his life after losing his wife, I leaned into it: "For many persons, the encounter with bereavement and grief can lead them to a more deeply meaningful and satisfying religious or spiritual life" (Tedeschi & Calhoun, 2006, p. 108). Because of the way my father transitioned, my faith only grew stronger after he died—in hindsight, my values and beliefs matched his story of loss. When pertaining to our way of life, "a study exploring a historical-cultural understanding of spirituality in India, identified 'union with the divine,' 'being at peace,' and 'preserving dignity' as the three core principles of spirituality at the end of life in India" (Inbadas, 2017, p. 338).

In the core of my heart, I felt that these three needs were met before my father died, and leading up to this death, we had a meaningful conversation in which he explained his wishes to *go there*, communicating his strong desire to *be with God*. Therefore, I could have no qualms or bitterness toward my faith or spirituality. *Dad's fate was as he wanted it to be.* Last, a spiritual practice that significantly contributed to my healing was through the fortification of my father's holy rite of passage, participating in ancient cultural mourning rituals. As Weller (2015) notes, "ritual elicits a certain vibration, a pitch that enables us to individually or communally connect with the sacred…it sutures the tears in the soul that occur in the daily rounds of living" (p. 78). Traditional rituals, which are laid out and explored in Chapter 4, brought the strength and support of my cultural community forward and allowed me to express the spiritual aspects of my grief that were otherwise not emphasized in modern western societies.

Nobel laureate and National Poet of India, Rabindranath Tagore, once penned, "Death is not extinguishing the light; it is only putting out the lamp because the dawn has come." By increasing my knowledge of the dawn, the broader metaphysical concepts surrounding death, I began to emerge from the dark wooded path. Slowly, an aperture of light appeared, shedding insight into the nature of my bereavement: *What is grief but a measure of the love I have for my father?* When faced with the intensity of my sorrow—the insurmountable heaviness, the fog that refused to lift, and the pain that would not cease—I remembered the true meaning behind my suffering. My grief was merely a direct reflection of the love I carry for my father. "My grief says that I dared to love, that I allowed another to enter the very core of my being and find a home in my heart" (Weller, 2015, p. 25). Now, my tears represent a form of spiritual cleansing, where each tear sheds in *honor of him*. Reframing my pain in this way brought the willpower and tenacity required to wake up each morning, begin anew, and face the endless adjustments and reminders that accompany loss. And, by closely examining the physical, social, psychological, behavioral, and spiritual responses that arose through my prolonged grief—I was ready to carry out the necessary grief work, aligning my reactions and responses in bereavement with grief theories and models that best suited my journey through the dark night of grief.

References

Adarkar, A., & Keiser, D. L. (2007). The buddha in the classroom: Toward a critical spiritual pedagogy. *Journal of Transformative Education, 5*(3), 246–261. https://doi.org/10.1177/1541344607306362

Aron, E. (1998). *The highly sensitive person: How to thrive when the world overwhelms you.* Harmony Books.

Attig, T. (1991). The importance of conceiving of grief as an active process. *Death Studies, 15*(4), 385–393. https://doi.org/10.1080/07481189108252443

Attig, T. (2011). *How we grieve: Relearning the world* (Rev. ed). Oxford University Press.

Attig, T. (2019). *Catching your breath in grief: -- And grace will lead you home.* Breath of Life Publishing.

Boelen, P. A., & Smid, G. E. (2017). The traumatic grief inventory self-report version (Tgi-sr): Introduction and preliminary psychometric evaluation. *Journal of Loss and Trauma, 22*(3), 196–212. https://doi.org/10.1080/15325024.2017.1284488

Bonanno, G. A. (2009). *The other side of sadness: What the new science of bereavement tells us about life after loss.* Basic Books.

Bowlby, J. (1961). Processes of Mourning. *The International Journal of Psycho-Analysis, 42*, 317–340.

Bowlby, J., & Bowlby, J. (1998). *Loss: Sadness and depression.* Pimlico.

Brussat, F., & Brussat, M. A. (1998). *Spiritual literacy: Reading the sacred in everyday life.* Touchstone.

Burnham, S. (2011). *The art of intuition: Cultivating your inner wisdom.* Jeremy P. Tarcher/Penguin.

Cacciatore, J. (2017). *Bearing the unbearable: Love, loss, and the heartbreaking path of grief.* Wisdom Publications.

Crotty, M. (1998). *The foundations of social research: Meaning and perspective in the research process.* Sage Publications.

Devine, M. (2017). *It's ok that you're not ok: Meeting grief and loss in a culture that doesn't understand.* Sounds True.

Doidge, N. (2007). *The brain that changes itself: Stories of personal triumph from the frontiers of brain science.* Penguin Books.

Doka, K. J. (2016). *Grief is a journey: Finding your path through loss.* Atria Books.

Hawley, J. (2011). *The Bhagavad Gita: A walkthrough for westerners.* New World Library.

Inbadas, H. (2017). The philosophical and cultural situatedness of spirituality at the end of life in India. *Indian Journal of Palliative Care, 23*(3), 338. https://doi.org/10.4103/IJPC.IJPC_61_17

Is broken heart syndrome real? (n.d.). Www.Heart.Org. Retrieved November 14, 2020, from https://www.heart.org/en/health-topics/cardiomyopathy/what-is-cardiomyopathy-in-adults/is-broken-heart-syndrome-real

Klass, D., & Steffen, E. (Eds.). (2018). *Continuing bonds in bereavement: New directions for research and practice.* Routledge, Taylor & Francis Group.

LaGrand, L. E. (2001). *Gifts from the unknown: Using extraordinary experiences to cope with loss and change.* Authors Choice Press.

Levine, P. A. (2015). *Trauma and memory: Brain and body in a search for the living past: a practical guide for under-*

standing and working with traumatic memory. North Atlantic Books.

Lewis, C. S. (1961). A grief observed. Bantam Books.

Lewis, T., Amini, F., & Lannon, R. (2001). A general theory of love (1. Vintage ed). Vintage.

Moore, T. (2004). Dark nights of the soul: A guide to finding your way through life's ordeals. Gotham Books.

Mosse, D. (1996). South Indian Christians, purity/impurity, and the caste system: Death ritual in a Tamil Roman Catholic community. The Journal of the Royal Anthropological Institute, 2(3), 461. https://doi.org/10.2307/3034898

Muller, W. (1993). Legacy of the heart: The spiritual advantages of a painful childhood (1. Fireside ed). Simon & Schuster.

Neimeyer, R. A. (2001). Meaning reconstruction & the experience of loss [Kindle version]. Retrieved from Amazon.com.

Parkes, C. M., & Prigerson, H. G. (2010). Bereavement: Studies of grief in adult life, fourth edition. Penguin Books.

Rando, T. (1993). Treatment of Complicated Mourning. Research Press.

Shear, M.K. (2012). Grief and mourning gone awry: Pathway and course of complicated grief. Dialogues in Clinical Neuroscience, 14(2), 119–128. https://doi.org/10.31887/DCNS.2012.14.2/mshear

Shear, M. K. (2015). Complicated grief. New England Journal of Medicine, 372(2), 153–160. https://doi.org/10.1056/NEJMcp1315618

Shulman, L. M. (2018). Before and after loss: A neurologist's perspective on loss, grief, and our brain. Johns Hopkins University Press.

Tedeschi, R. G., & Calhoun, L. G. (2006). Time of change? The spiritual challenges of bereavement and loss. OMEGA - Journal of Death and Dying, 53(1), 105–116. https://doi.org/10.2190/7MBU-UFV9-6TJ6-DP83

Van der Kolk, B. (2014). The body keeps the score. Penguin Books.

Weller, F. (2015). The wild edge of sorrow: Rituals of renewal and the sacred work of grief. North Atlantic Books.

Wolfelt, A. (2003). Understanding your grief: Ten essential touchstones for finding hope and healing your heart. Companion Press.

Wolfelt, A. (2014). The depression of grief: Coping with your sadness and knowing when to get help. Companion Press.

Worden, J.W. (2018). Grief Counseling and grief therapy: A handbook for the mental health practitioner. Springer Publishing Company, LLC.

Chapter 3

CARRYING OUT GRIEF WORK

A Closer Look at Grief Theories and Models

I did not know the work of mourning

Is like carrying a bag of cement

Up a mountain at night

The mountaintop is not in sight

Because there is no mountaintop

Poor Sisyphus grief

—Edward Hirsch, *Gabriel*

After the heroic phase of grief had passed, the dust had settled, and the social support had vanished, I became paralyzed by fear, or in C.S. Lewis's (1961) astute observation—paralyzed by *grief*. A scholar at heart, the moment an ounce of energy returned, I began reading, researching, and absorbing all I could find on the topic of death and grief. The first instructional book that caught my eye was Dr. Wolfelt's (2016) *When Your Soulmate Dies*. I flipped through the pages, and phrases such as "twin flames" (p. 10) *that's what I called us* or "two peas in a pod" (p. 5) *that's what he called us* jumped off the page. I decided that this must be the right guide to lessen my grief. I read the book within an hour, and though I felt comfort, I knew it was not enough—that it was only the beginning of my grief work. According to Stroebe and Schut (2010),

Grief work is understood to refer to the cognitive process of confronting the reality of a loss through death, of going over events that occurred before and at the time of death, and of focusing on memories and working toward detachment from (or relocating) the deceased. (p. 275)

Consciously working through my grief helped me to adapt to the ongoing changes that accompanied my loss, as even after the emotional aspects of bereavement subsided, my neural networks still needed to process that his death had occurred (Doidge, 2007).

Mourners have ample choice of grief theories and models that will support them in better understanding their grief and adjusting to bereavement. Parkes (1998) explains that "a model is a way of describing and categorizing phenomena, it does not explain them; a theory on the other hand implies explanation and, to some extent, causation" (p. 21). Grief researchers such as Attig, Bowlby, Doka, Freud, Klass, Kübler-Ross, Neimeyer, Parkes, Prigerson, Rando, Schut, Silverman, Stroebe, Wolfelt, and Worden are well-known for their immense contributions to developing our knowledge of grief. A key component of grief literature summarizes their theories and discusses the various process models that emerged from them. This chapter will provide a brief overview of the history and evolution of the underlying themes that have shaped grief theories, closely examining four coping models that have supplemented my knowledge and understanding of successful healing.

The Models of Grief

As my grief became insufferable, I had no choice but to engage in conscious grief work to cope with the loss of my father. *Coping* throughout one's bereavement refers to:

Processes, strategies, or styles of managing (reducing, mastering, tolerating) the situation in which bereavement places the individual. Coping is assumed to impact on adaptation to bereavement. If coping is effective, then not only the suffering, but also the mental and physical ill health difficulties that are associated with bereavement…should be reduced. (Stroebe & Schut, 2010, p. 274)

Even though I began actively grieving soon after my father's death, coping with his loss only occurred two years later, after enduring the many trials and errors of seeking effective grief support. The road to finding successful interventions that alleviate griever suffering has not been smooth, partly because the rationale shaping earlier grief theories assumed that grief can be cured through a standardized approach. In his essay, *Mourning and Melancholia* (1917), Sigmund Freud laid the foundation for a theory that would solidify a false understanding of grief work that still lingers today. That is, in order "for successful mourning to take place, the mourner must disengage from the deceased, let go of the past, and move on" (Klass & Steffen, 2018, p. 3). As touched upon earlier, it was not until his daughter Sophie died that Freud realized his inaccuracies, which is evident in a letter of consolation that he wrote to his friend, Ludwig Binswanger, after he suffered a similar fate of losing a child:

> Although we know that after such a loss the acute state of mourning will subside, we also know we shall remain inconsolable and will never find a substitute. No matter what may fill the gap, even if it be filled completely, it nevertheless remains something else. And actually this is how it should be. It is the only way of perpetuating the love we do not want to relinquish. (Freud, 1961, as cited in Klass et al., 1996, p. 6)

Yet, this realization had come too late, as the notion of the necessity of detaching from the deceased had already irreversibly penetrated our psychological understanding of grief work. *Is this why people tell me it's important to move on?* It is a subconscious, disengaged, and lazy effort from others—contrived by a person who renounced his own ideas. According to more recent and current grief theories and models, moving on is no longer an acceptable or accurate remedy for grief.

Earlier grief models demonstrated grieving as a set order of events that traveled in a straight line through stages, phases, or patterns. Bonanno (2009) suggests that the appeal for using a stage model is that "it serves as a neat and tidy way to think about grieving. It provides a comforting outline of what people might expect while they are going through difficult times" (p. 22). However, grief, in its pure state, is anything but clear-cut. And even though these models could apply in some cases, they were not meant to be universal and were pushed on the grieving community. Klass and Steffen (2018) argue that the "dominant Western model of grief did not account for important aspects of the experiences of bereaved people" (p. 2). Grief is much more complex than consistently adhering to set stages, or "rigid parameters for 'proper' behaviour that do not match what most people go through" (Bonanno, 2009, p. 22), nor do these borders address the individuality of the griever. As Attig (1991) notes, these models "suggest that there is little choice of paths through the process" (p. 386). Thus, viewing grief work through a linear lens encourages passivity, even though we now know the importance of actively participating in the grieving process and shaping the work to fit the needs of the mourner: "emphasizing the active and potentially life-enhancing character of the coping process motivates the bereaved to invest the energy required for change and life transformation" (Attig, 1991, p. 392).

Grief work requires a multifaceted approach to authentically reconcile the loss, taking into account the survivor's unique reactions and responses to grief as they arise. A coping model that works well for one individual may not benefit another. Or, as in my case, differentiating, selecting, and combining elements from different theories and models was the most helpful approach I could take to heal effectively. To surmount the obstacles that occur when grieving and detach from the opinions ingrained within the dominant culture, I had to educate myself on the evolution of grief theories and seek out more current models, permitting myself to *break the rules* of bereavement. And while many helpful grief theories exist, the four scientific models that interacted with my prolonged grief early on, both culturally and individually, were: The Five Stages of Grief, Dual Process Model of Coping with Bereavement, Tasks of Mourning, and Continuing Bonds.

The Five Stages of Grief

I am the master of my fate, I am the captain of my soul.

—William Ernest Henley, *Invictus*

In 1969, Elisabeth Kübler-Ross, an esteemed pioneer of grief work, released the Stages of the Grief Cycle. This model established grief as a linear process that journeys through five stages: *denial and isolation, anger, bargaining, depression,* and eventually, *acceptance.* I was well aware of this cycle before my loss and most likely believed these stages as valid. However, after experiencing death more intimately and understanding how inaccurate this model was, I began to read more about it. Here, I learned how Dr. Kübler-Ross created the stages based on her observations of patients dying from terminal illnesses within a hospice. Her theory was structured to measure the acceptance of one's own death, but instead became an established framework for survivors of loss. Soon, criticism and backlash arose from grievers and researchers because grief is not a passive process, nor does it operate under a predictable, one-size-fits-all model. Corr (2015) argues to *stop staging grief*, stating, "there are no grounds to believe that humans are limited to no more than five ways of reacting and responding...[and] early empirical research from the 1970s did not provide support for this model" (p. 227). Although misconstrued, The Five Stages of Grief continued to gather steam because the one-way track of navigating grief was straightforward and easy to follow—mostly for those outside of the mourning process.

In their book, *On Grief and Grieving*, Kübler-Ross and Kessler (2005) explain how the stages are "very misunderstood...they were never meant to help tuck messy emotions into neat packages...there is no typical response to loss, as there is no typical loss" (p. 7). They state that the intention behind the stages was to provide coping tools for grief by framing and identifying feelings that *may* arise within loss. However, the Kübler-Ross's Grief Cycle became so ingrained in the counseling profession that "even if the five stages are not explicitly mentioned, they underlie so much of what counselors and doctors think of as the 'healthy' way to grieve" (Devine, 2017, p. 30). And these stages are so rooted in our daily interactions that those who lag in reaching acceptance are viewed as unhealthy mourners.

I often found those around me subconsciously laying out the process: *What stage are you in now? Oh, you're angry today; you must have hit that stage. Don't worry denial is part of the stages, it will pass.* I soon understood that I could travel through all five stages in the course of one day, and then the next, and the next. Thus, my main criticism of this model is that it gave more power to the non-griever to direct the grieving process rather than empowering the individual experiencing it. As helpful and as structured as Kübler-Ross's (1969) model tried to be, it was being misused as a linear tool to manage and restrict the chaotic and explosive nature of grief. Thus, newer and more realistic models and theories for processing grief appeared. And, despite that many models have developed since Kübler-Ross's, a popular tool used in grief counseling today is Stroebe and Schut's (2010) Dual Process Model of Coping with Bereavement.

Dual Process Model of Coping with Bereavement

> In the cycle of nature there is no such thing as victory or defeat; there is only movement.

—Paulo Coelho, *Manuscript Found in Accra*

The Dual Process Model of Coping with Bereavement (DPM) was created by Margaret Stroebe and Henk Schut "as an alternative to stage-based models of human grief" (Jeffreys, 2011, p. 75). This model made a sound argument that grief does not travel in a straight line but is an ongoing oscillation between the loss-orientation side (dwelling on and searching for what has been lost) and the restoration-orientation side (learning how to live again without what was lost). It was the first scientific theory to account for the ongoing movement of grief directly in the model: "Oscillation is *key* to this theory, as it is a regulatory process that makes coping effective and makes this model unique from previous theories such as phases or tasks" (Worden, 2018, p. 55). DPM also integrates interpersonal factors and embeds space for grievers to pause and rest from continuously laboring through grief work. Stroebe and Schut (2010) explain how their model (see Figure 1) supports the unpredictable and irrational behavior of grief:

> The principle underlying oscillation is that at times the bereaved will confront aspects of loss, at other times avoid them, and the same applies to the tasks of restoration. Sometimes, too, there will be "time out," when the person is not grieving. Coping with bereavement according to the DPM is thus a complex regulatory process of confrontation and avoidance. An important postulation of the model is that oscillation between the two types of stressors is necessary for adaptive coping. (p. 278)

The DPM was first introduced to me in grief counseling and paved the way for an authentic path toward healing because it "provides a framework for understanding forms of *complicated grief*" (Stroebe & Schut, 2010, p. 281). In contrast to other theories, this model was more reliable and accepting of my chronic reactions to a life-changing loss. The "dynamic coping process" (Stroebe & Schut, 2010, p. 278), or oscillating element of describing grief, diminished the pressure I placed on myself to complete grieving by permitting me to not need to finish it.

Throughout the earlier upheavals of bereavement, the DPM relayed a simple and manageable approach to tackling grief while still allowing the griever entitlement over their responses. I even began correcting those who told me, *I should be at the acceptance stage by now*, by educating them on the more current model, reinforcing that they were following outdated, harmful practices. And, when this framework was laid out in front of them and explained using a visual of the scientific model, they easily followed the reasoning behind the ongoing dynamic of grief.

Figure 1

Dual Process Model of Coping with Bereavement

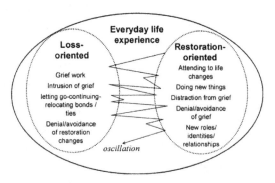

Note. Reprinted with permission from Stroebe, M., & Schut, H. (2010). The dual process model of coping with bereavement: A decade on. *OMEGA - Journal of Death and Dying, 61*(4), 273–289.

Even though the DPM speaks to the non-linear nature of grief, I sometimes felt conflicted navigating situations that simultaneously fit under both the loss-oriented side and the restoration-oriented side (for example, a wedding). Perhaps expanding on a third, transition-oriented facet may be beneficial, exploring those obscure, liminal spaces when the bereaved find themselves in the middle. Nevertheless, once reasonable steps towards reconciliation were taken using this dynamic processing model and some relief was felt, I was then able to shift to a task-based model that required greater mental strength and stamina to confront grief's complexities. These theories and models should work in unison with each other, not pitted against one another, as compiling the strengths of each will only further expand the toolkit needed to support the intricate suffering of the griever. Thus, once the DPM brought stability to my recovery, I moved into the Tasks of Mourning, which helped compartmentalize my grief work.

Tasks of Mourning

For you, a thousand times over.

—Khaled Hosseini, *The Kite Runner*

As an adolescent, I watched my father through a heart attack and open-heart surgery that was complicated and almost led to his demise. Being a teenager, I was not equipped to deal with the intensity of such trauma, so I withdrew and avoided processing the pain altogether. However, Worden (2018) insists that "it is necessary to acknowledge and work through this pain or it can manifest itself through physical symptoms or some form of aberrant behavior" (p. 45). And in my twenties, I discovered the repercussions of hidden stress that materialized after my abandonment of this major life event (Maté, 2012). Masked feelings resurfaced as a series of panic attacks, extreme insomnia, and severe emotional pain. Seeking help from a psychologist, the unexpected physical symptoms and buried mental distress were retraced back to the event of his heart attack. The timing of the deterioration of my own health directly correlated to his, from ten years prior. I had become a practical life lesson of Van der Kolk's (2014) book, *The Body Keeps the Score*, where he explains how traumatic experiences are remembered at the cellular level. Thus, when my father died, I was adamant not to repeat past blunders. Almost immediately after his death, I consciously began processing the pain. And, subconsciously, I believe that I was carrying out Worden's (2018) Tasks of Mourning: *to accept the reality of the loss, to process the pain of grief, to adjust to a world without the deceased,* and *to find a way to remember the deceased while embarking on the rest of one's journey through life.*

Task I – To Accept the Reality of the Loss. Early in the mourning process, my acceptance of the reality of my father's death was unclear. I transitioned through a phase of "middle knowledge…both knowing and not knowing at the same time" (Worden, 2018, p. 44). Repeating phrases or communicating that *he died* seemed impossible at first. However, as heart-rending as it was, the more I deliberately spoke of his death, the more I accepted the reality of the loss. After the traditional funeral had passed, I performed a series of final ceremonies, rituals, and prayers established within my eastern heritage. These spiritual tasks all contributed to my understanding of the finality of death, providing a firmer grip on the reality of loss, increasing my cognitive awareness around communal interactions. With completing each measure of cyclical rituals, a greater acceptance of his death ensued. The intellectual understanding of death was easier for me to master; however, the emotional acceptance only appeared later on as I moved through the other three tasks.

Task II – To Process the Pain of Grief. Since I was proactive with my suffering, I initiated clinical care soon after he died. I scheduled appointments with my psychologist, I contacted grief counseling centers and support groups, and I even volunteered with the local hospice to support children and teens who had lost a parent. The more I surrounded myself with those who grieved and professionals who dealt with grief, the more I processed the pain effectively. During the day, I could feel the ferocity of the emotional waves stirring internally. Thus, when I was alone in the evenings, I followed a consistent regime. Sitting in complete darkness, propped up on my father's chair, I held onto his belongings and felt through the pain of losing him. I had to make meaning of the items and their loss of identity also. With a selected playlist of my father's favorite songs spinning in the background, I permitted myself to *cry it out*: "Stress causes chemical imbalances in the body, and some researchers believe that tears remove toxic substances and help re-establish homeostasis" (Worden, 2018, p. 30). Apart from sitting still and surrendering to his loss, I also acted on intuitive inklings that nudged me. I drew grief maps, wrote letters, and constructed a photo album of my father's last days, all of which helped me to find order in the chaos of grief. Eventually, this led to writing out the detailed stories of his death, and storytelling processed the events, restoring my health through disclosure (Pennebaker, 2000). The more time I dedicated to intentionally mourning, the lighter the weight of my grief became.

Task III – To Adjust to a World Without the Deceased. Adjusting to a world without my father was the most difficult task for me to face and come to terms with. According to Worden (2018), "the survivor usually is not aware of all the roles played by the deceased until sometime after the loss occurs" (p. 47). My father was such a crucial figure in my life that the parts he played were innumerable, many of which only became apparent after he died. Hence, the adjustments I had to make were endless and often too heartbreaking to handle. Worden (2018) explains that:

> There are *external adjustments*, or how the death affects one's everyday functioning in the world; *internal adjustments*, or how the death affects one's sense of self; and *spiritual adjustments*, or how the death affects one's beliefs, values, and assumptions about the world. (p. 47)

For the most part, internal and spiritual adjustments were a lone endeavor. However, externally, my family had to adjust from being a nice, even square to a disproportionate triangle. Because of our personality traits and differences in mourning styles, this adjustment did not come easy. As cliché as it may sound, *Dad was the glue that held us together*, knowing each of us intimately and catering to our needs simultaneously. Worden (2018) supports that "most families exist in some type of homeostatic balance, and the loss of a significant person in the family group can unbalance this homeostasis and cause the family to feel pain" (p. 217). This external adjustment took both time and consistent effort to more deeply understand each other's struggles. For us, the change of family dynamics was "taxing…generate[d] friction and misunderstanding, and…produce[d] strong emotion" (Bonanno, 2009, p. 34). Frequently, our grief, the ache of losing him, was painfully released on one another.

After our issues settled, reparation was evident, and we slowly adapted to our life as a smaller family unit. Using my other family members as a crutch, I ultimately learned how to distribute the support in my life more evenly. I matched certain characteristics of my father with specific people and selectively turned to these individuals as needed. Yet, no matter how many adjustments I made to replace the key person in my life, *nobody was quite like him*. Eventually, I became aware of the importance of learning the fourth task, securing a connection with my father while still moving forward with my life.

Task IV – To Find a Way to Remember the Deceased While Embarking on the Rest of One's Journey Through Life. With the ongoing deterioration of my health, the fourth task became the most crucial for me to master to reconstruct a positive sense of well-being. Shortly after he died—*remembering my father*—was essential for both me and those around me. But as time went on, the memory that he once existed seemed to vanish for others. At first, stories of him stopped circulating in our social circles, and then, for a significant period, his name was not mentioned at all. I knew the underlying reason was to not remind us of our loss; however, *would any outside force ever stop me from thinking of my dad?* No. Often, I found myself repeating the phrase, *he still matters*, throughout the day. Unconsciously, I talked about my father from morning until night. When others viewed my dialogue as unhealthy, they tried to stifle my speech—and temporarily succeeded. But then I was reminded that, before he died, I talked about my dad to no end—*why should that change now?* Worden (2018) affirms that "we now know that people do not decathect from the dead but find ways to remember the deceased" (p. 50). Because of their discomfort, I was muted. However, once I found a way past their wall of treachery, I resisted giving into misinformed views, and purposefully, I kept him alive in my conversations. I was determined to let others know that my dad was still very much a part of my life—*a part of me.*

According to Shear (2012),

> Mourning is the process by which bereaved people seek and find ways to turn the light on in the world again…when successful, mourning leads people to feel deeply connected to deceased loved ones while also able to imagine a satisfying future without them. (p. 121)

For my family, finding a way to remember the deceased while embarking on the rest of our journeys through life happened on individual and group levels. We developed new routines that continued to honor the *head of our household* still—visiting my father's grave, lighting candles, leaving fresh flowers by his picture. These *rituals of affirmation* that "allow us to say thank-you for the legacies we have received from the deceased" (Doka, 2016, p. 235), not only created a more cohesive unit among the three of us, but also helped us feel that our family of four was still united and present. On the individual level, I strengthened and sustained my connection with my father through the work I have set out to do in memory of him. And the achievements that stem from this work prove my mourning has been successful, and my life is moving forward gracefully.

The last theoretical framework discussed in this chapter, Continuing Bonds (Klass et al., 1996; Klass & Steffen, 2018), relates to Worden's fourth task. As a griever, learning to process my grief by continuing a relationship with the deceased was a strength. And since CB was the most prominent model I used, I have separated it into its own section. Here, I will discuss how continuing the relationship with my father enabled me to reap positive benefits in my grief and moved me closer to reconciliation. In my eyes, CB is a powerful processing model that continues to provide me with a strong sense of relief and deep healing daily. I know by embedding CB rituals in my life every day, my father remains ever-present with me.

Continuing Bonds

> I tried to explain that I am not without you, that you are with me from the moment I wake until the moment I fall asleep, that it's you I feel when the wind caresses me, that it's your voice I hear in the silence, you whom I see when I close my eyes, you who makes me laugh and sing when I know no one else is around.

—Jan-Philipp Sendker, *The Art of Hearing Heartbeats*

My father had just died, and I finished spending the first few days of mourning attached to my mother and brother. Upon returning to my apartment, I finally sat with a moment of silence, the solitude I needed to catch my breath in loss. Suddenly, while drowned in an unspeakable amount of pain, I had an experience that can only be explained as an encounter with enlightenment, "a state of connectedness with something immeasurable and indestructible, something that, almost paradoxically, is essentially you and yet is much greater than you" (Tolle, 1999, p. 12). During the most pivotal crossroad of my life, a knowing, an inexplicable wave of energy washed over me. I heard within myself the following statement: *If you are as close to your father as you claim to be, then the true nature of your relationship starts now.* I didn't question it; I heard the message loud and clear: "What is it that separated us? Only the illusion of identity – only the illusion of separateness" (Taylor, 2015, p. 58). From this momentous awakening onward, I decided that continuing the bond with my father was not only necessary for my survival—it was essential to my evolution as a spiritual being.

Encouraged through my Indian roots, it is not abnormal to maintain ties with the deceased; culturally, spiritual manifestations of departed family members are welcomed and talked about openly, and inexplicable sensory perceptions link to the presence or protection of spiritual ancestors. Klass et al. (1996) reinforce that,

> As the modern Western world has moved toward a more and more autonomous and individualistic definition of the self, it has tended toward valuing 'reality-based' behaviour that precludes acknowledging any ongoing relationship with the deceased. Most other cultures in the history seem to have supported the notion that the deceased continue to live in some form after death, and they provide mourners with rituals to sustain an appropriate relationship. (p. 19–20).

Because of my traditional upbringing, I did not have to work through the unknown to be open to the process. As a child, I had had such experiences with both of my grandfathers appearing to me through dream visitations which taught me that "attachment does not cease when a loved person dies" (Parkes & Prigerson, 2010, p. 68). Thus, exploring a sustained connection with my father was not an uncomfortable task for me; it came naturally and was a relatively organic transition. Genuinely, I was magnetized to the idea, and intuitively, *I already knew what to do.* Alongside this deep knowing, before he died, my father left me with remarkable wisdom on how to cope: *Linita, physically, I will no longer be here, but spiritually, I am always with you.* The firmness in his voice and the security of his stare can be recalled in an instant. With one sentence, he emboldened me to listen carefully and follow the advice he was sincerely trying to tell me, that: "a bond with the deceased continues, but also changes the multi-dimensional bond with the living person" (Klass & Steffen, 2018, p. 4). My father held me accountable for my actions even after he was gone, creating a need for me to stay persistent with my healing. And so, taking his words directly to heart, this phrase alone brought me through to the other side of grief, as this phrase alone led me to seek out ways to continue our bond.

Klass and Steffen (2018) explain that when continuing bonds, "bereaved people did not sever the bonds with significant people who had died as the accepted theory said they should. Rather, people continued the attachment albeit in new circumstances" (p. xiii). Despite that CB was once deemed taboo and widely questioned as a beneficial grief theory in the past, it is now more accepted and recognized as a valuable contributor to understanding a healthy mourning process. However, there are distinctions that need to be taken into consideration. Field and Filanosky (2009) elaborate on the usefulness of CB by creating two distinct expressions, internalized (integrates loss) and externalized (inhibits reconciliation):

> We distinguish externalized CB expressions involving illusions and hallucinations of the deceased, indicative of unresolved loss as it defined in the adult attachment literature, from internalized CB expressions involving use of mental representation of the deceased as a secure base that may serve to facilitate integration of the loss. (p. 2)

This grief model might not be suited for all individuals, as moderating variables such as violent loss, feeling responsible for the loss, static healing, or clinging to the deceased without actively seeking reconciliation, are factors that can lead to unhealthy expressions of CB. Also, a determinant that could disrupt or inhibit the efficacy of this model are the cultural conditions surrounding the griever, as "many bereaved people actually experience a strong, perceptible connection with deceased loved ones…but Western cultural norms about scientific objectivity may also make them deeply unsettling" (Bonanno, 2009, p. 9). Thus, due to my personality traits, my desire to engage in constructive meaning-making, my ability to "establish psychological proximity to the deceased through use of the deceased as an internalized secure base" (Field & Filanosky, 2009, p. 4), and my cultural context—continuing bonds easily embedded themselves into my grieving process in a reparative way.

Continuing Bonds Through Actions

I inhale, and you are there.

I exhale, and you are also there.

Those who assume we must separate,

Must not know the value of air.

—Linita Eapen Mathew, *Air*

Before my father died, I used to call him twice a day, every day. If I had important news to share or something substantial had occurred, he was the first to hear. Every conscious decision I made took him into account and was finalized by his input. And so, it was agonizingly difficult adjusting to a world with no compass. Without him, I lost all sight of direction. Thus, in the aftermath of his death, I began writing letters to him—*Letters from a Broken-hearted Daughter*—and I wrote to him religiously. The words in these letters penned a path to my father, updating him on my thoughts, feelings, and major life events. In this way, writing letters played "a positive part in the [survivor's] ongoing [life]" (Klass & Steffen, 2018, p. xiii) by providing my dad with the ability to continue participating in it.

My father instilled in me the value of *honoring thy father and mother*. Moving into my adulthood, I gladly adhered to this form of respect, not because I had to, but because I wanted to. As per our customs, I sought permission from both of my parents before embarking on any new adventure in my life, small or large. This practice was not always understood by my western friends, especially as I got older. However, it was my firm belief that if I did not receive my father's blessings, I would not meet my target or accomplish what I set out to do. Even now, I believe, *I am succeeding because my father has blessed me*: "Phenomena that indicate active continuing bonds are a sense of presence…belief in the person's continuing active influence on thoughts or events, or a conscious incorporation of the characteristics or virtues of the dead into the self" (Klass & Steffen, 2018, p. 4).

In India, the Hindu religion promotes acquiring blessings by touching an elder's feet and then touching one's own heart, signifying that the lowliest part of the elder's body is equivalent to the most vital part of the younger generation. Even though we are Christians, I loved touching my father's feet and taking his blessings; it reminded me of the enormous reverence I held for him. Before leaving the hospital room the night he died, I held onto his feet firmly, unable to let go. His feet were the last part of him that I touched, requesting his protection as I transitioned into a new life. This traditional practice was important to me, one I needed to continue past his death. Klass and Steffen (2018) support that "at a micro level, meanings can also be seen as depending on the nature and history of the relationship with the deceased who is still present and alive for the bereaved" (p. 9). Hence, for everyday obeisance, I light a candle and touch my hand to his picture, and for larger life decisions, I visit the cemetery and touch the ground of his resting place. Auspicious markers such as these have increased my ability to relearn my ties with the deceased. As Field and Filanosky (2009) note, through these internalized expressions of CB, "she can imagine the deceased's viewpoint on practical matters and use this as a guide in making decisions or treating the deceased as an ideal to emulate" (p. 4).

Lastly, the most evident act of service is this book, a clear example of post-traumatic growth (Calhoun & Tedeschi, 2001), in which I have continued the bond with my father through a mission to serve:

> The mission might be to educate the public, or to support others going through similar circumstances. These missions of service are often accomplished in the name of the deceased person, and in that sense also represent a continuing bond. This bond is one of honor and remembrance. It helps keep this person alive and the name used and can represent a furthering of the life narrative of the deceased person as well as the bereaved person. In this way, the bereaved person carries their loved one into the future as a living force for good and as a partner in making the world a better place. (Klass & Steffen, 2018, p. 39)

Continuing Bonds Through Extraordinary Experiences

Yes I know, this is nothing but thy love, O beloved of my heart – this golden light that dances upon the leaves, these idle clouds sailing across the sky, this passing breeze leaving its coolness upon my forehead. The morning light has flooded my eyes – this is thy message to my heart. Thy face is bent from above, thy eyes look down on my eyes, and my heart has touched thy feet.

—Rabindranath Tagore, *Gitanjali*

In his book, *Gifts from the Unknown: Using Extraordinary Experiences to Cope with Loss and Change*, Louis LaGrand (2001) describes how the grieving community is known to receive unexplained forms of communication from their deceased loved ones, such as: *a sense of presence, dream visitations, sensory (visual, auditory, olfactory, and tactile), symbolic*, and *third-party experiences*. The author explains that these types of non-verbal forms of communication, although they have a clear purpose in the mourning process, are not always readily accepted in our society:

> This curious discarding of subjective experience occurs because we live in a culture dominated by physical reality and scientific materialism. When secular wisdom reigns supreme, the philosophical and the spiritual become a turn-off for many, and so too is the extraordinary experience because we are directly taught not to recognize the validity of realities that cannot be proved by the seeing-is-believing ethic. We forget that sense experience alone is not the true test of reality; our senses are inadequate for the job of understanding the full picture, even though we are told to rely on them exclusively. Nevertheless, the consistent appearance of the extraordinary and the unexpected, especially when one is in need, is a puzzling hallmark of life. (p. 4)

Multiple authors have noted that grievers often report having experienced these supernatural occurrences—seeing, hearing, or feeling the presence of a loved one (Klass & Steffen, 2018; Parkes & Prigerson, 2010). LaGrand's book itself was written to account for the commonality of these manifestations among the bereaved. He wanted to give the grieving community a better understanding of how to decipher transcendent experiences, teaching them how to engage with the emergence of metaphysical encounters wholly to encourage the arrival of such gifts throughout the mourning process. Similarly, LaGrand (2001) references the survivor's ability to have an intuitive experience in unison with the demise, as some "report the sense of presence at or near the moment of death *before* they have been officially notified of the death" (p. 6). For me, this was true, as moments before my father died, I heard him call out to me twice in our native tongue, Malayalam: *Daughter, wake up*. I smiled to myself, wondering why I had heard him, not knowing the nurse was already on her way in to deliver earth-shattering news.

I was well-versed in deciphering deeply personal, non-verbal messages found in my surroundings even before my father's death. The eastern worldview relies heavily on symbolism and divine order, though most western interpretations refer to them as "coincidence, chance, occurrences…nothing but wishful thinking, [and] a form of deception" (LaGrand, 2001, p. 5). Yet, I am a meaning-maker, a supporter of Frankl's (2006) reasoning behind logotherapy, or *man's will to find meaning* in human existence. And for most of my twenties, I learned how to make sense of my environment and spiritually interact with it. Due to this prior practice, I was more than willing and capable of decoding my father's new form of non-verbal language. I knew that he loved philosophy and all things related to nature, specifically, daffodils and butterflies. When the first spring arrived after his passing, *as luck would have it*, daffodils bloomed directly in front of my parking stall. It would be my first sighting of a real daffodil up until this point in my life. *This has to be him.* Likewise, when I was in India, white butterflies noticeably danced across my path or rested on the wall to the right of me. *That's obviously him.* Or, an old song my father loved played on three separate occasions in three separate stores, just as my foot hit the threshold. *It's definitely him.*

When a more direct message was essential, I would hear my father's voice clearly guiding me through some form of natural, telepathic conversation. Like a chinook wind on a cold day, his advice would brush past and warm me. Or, when faced with difficult decisions, unexpectedly, one of my father's philosophical sayings would pop up on the television, radio, or from a third-party person in the room, causing me to acknowledge that: *that's what Dad would have said.* LaGrand (2001) supports my experience, stating,

> Hearing the voice of the deceased or other sounds related exclusively to the loved one is also a fairly common event...sometimes the voice is heard as in a normal conversation, at other times it comes through as a mind to mind or telepathic communication. (p. 8)

Last, numbers provided a pivotal form of communication between me and my father, specifically the numbers associated with his birthday, *January 5,* his death anniversary, *January 14,* and the time of his death, *1:41.* When important events occurred in my life, they would fall on the 5th or the 14th of the month. For instance, I was accepted into the doctorate program *on the fifth,* and I received notification of funding for the program *on the fourteenth.*

Understandably, interacting with extraordinary experiences will not align with nor match each individual's forte. However, one who is grieving is raw, vulnerable, and pierced by the existential dread that accompanies death. Being open to these spiritual gifts, as presented here, may produce astounding, alleviating results. In the end, whether these occurrences were flukes or coincidences did not matter or take precedence in my mind. What mattered was that they brought me a sense of comfort and higher awareness that my father was still with me and that the bond that we shared never ceased existing.

Dream Visitations

I think we dream so we don't have to be apart for so long. If we're in each other's dreams, we can be together all the time.

—A.A. Milne, *Winnie-the-Pooh*

Dream visitations are a common experience among the bereaved. A dream sequence involving the deceased can be a vital part of adjusting to bereavement and moving toward reconciliation. Black et al. (2020) have shown that dreams "actively function to help the dreamer process grief" (p. 20) and can assist with continuing bonds with the deceased, supporting emotional regulation, and processing trauma. And, after a person has died, dream visitations can also fill in the gaps left by the missing person in small, yet consoling ways, such as saying a proper goodbye.

> The dream visit by the deceased is among the most common yet deeply comforting experience that often has a dramatic effect on the mourner. Problems have been solved, love given and received, and unfinished business taken care of. Dream visits commonly give reassurance that the loved one is whole, happy and in a beautiful place. (LaGrand, 2001, p. 12)

Not only do grief researchers see grief dreams as helpful, but they also recognize that these dreams can act as indicators for the bereaved as to where they are in the grieving process. When I analyzed my dreams after my father's death, the immediate visions resembled graphic night terrors. I was always back in the hospital, fighting for him to live, and shaken awake by a tragic ending. Parkes and Prigerson (2010) report that "it is no surprise to find that bereaved dreamers continue to go over in their minds the vivid mental images that preoccupy their waking hours and, out of them, create the action, setting and cast of their dreams" (p. 73). Thus, early in my grieving, scenes and scenarios of stressful events that had occurred in the hospital repeated nightly. This is because sufferers of PTSD are likely to have nightmares until the event is processed, and "such dreams should be treated as potential indicators of psychological distress" (Black et al., 2020, p. 21). I could feel the tragedy replaying in my mind, giving rise to anxieties that I felt in my chest. As a result, I often woke in a panic, drenched in sweat, gasping for air, reaching for a father who was no longer there. Yet, oddly enough, seeing him for those brief moments also provided simultaneous relief—I was relieved to see him still alive.

As I continued to trek down the path of prolonged grief and sought ways to actively grieve and heal, my dreams noticeably shifted in positive ways—when my condition improved, so did his. Slowly, different types of visions started to appear. I've had lucid dreams, where I've interacted with him directly; I've had observational dreams, where I sat back and noticed how healthy he looks; and I've had meaningful dreams, where a message was relayed by the end of our visit. Out of all the visitations I have had from my father, the following stands out the most:

> Carrying out my normal routine, I ran upstairs to Dad's room, eager to see him. Intrusively, my mind spoke to me, "He won't be there, Linita. He died." Ignoring my conscience, I kept climbing the long staircase anyway. Finally, I reached the top of the steps and turned left toward his bedroom; a feeling of fear and excitement mingled into one. Entering, I looked to find him standing in front of me, waiting for me. His form was not the same as before, it was different, almost abstract, but I knew it was him—his energy exuded from it. Dad looked healthier, fuller, and lighter than he had ever looked in his physical form. He took my arm and sat me next to him, placing my head on the rise of his belly, just like before. He patted my head, comforting me, his universal sign to let me know all is well. Suddenly, I noticed the condition of his feet. I had routinely spent my time putting diabetic lotion on his legs. I knew the shape and state of his feet better than anyone. Yet, here, his feet were soft and glowing; not a single crack defined the condition of his skin. Amazed, I reached down to touch them, to make sure they were real—that he was real. My brain fired off a signal, waking me in an instant. Our extraordinary experience had come to an end.

Although I have had many dreams of my father since his death, this was one of the more vivid and lucid instances. I was fully aware of each moment, and my mind was equally involved. I even awoke because the interaction was too painful to process, knowing that I could not stay with him once I opened my eyes. This specific dream came after an agonizing day of grieving when I missed my father immensely and needed to feel his comforting touch. Thus, I do believe his visitation came through intentionally as a symbolic source of solace. Klass and Steffen (2018) state that, "dreams of an ideal life…were experienced as comforting by the bereaved, as they were interpreted to signify the deceased's smooth transition to a quality afterlife" (p. 280). For me, the condition of his feet represented the removal of the pain and suffering caused by his physical body while he was alive. Wherever he was, he was safe.

As discovered in my dream visitations, the deceased can come through as a means of bringing closure to the distress caused by the death of a loved one, encouraging the bereaved to continue on their journey toward recovery. As I reconciled with my loss, the panic, fear, and trauma of experiencing the death of a loved one—were replaced with vitality, vibrancy, and a welcomed perspective. Now, dream visitations are understood to be opportunities that allow me to spend a few more moments with my father still. And for that, I am thankful. Moving into a place of acceptance, and knowing that my father is readily available in my dreams, brings forth a gratitude and joy that can exist in grief.

The Evolving Griever

The four grief models explored in this chapter sporadically appeared in my first year of bereavement. Yet, evolving as a griever occurs on a steep learning curve, and this path is infinite and unrestrainable by prescribed methods. After my father died, my world became desolate, barren, and meaningless. Thus, constructivist theories such as meaning reconstruction (Neimeyer, 2001) and relearning my place in the world (Attig, 2011) were equally crucial to my recovery, suturing the identity-shattering aspects of losing a loved one. And, even though these grief theories were not discussed at length in this chapter, they are profoundly visible in the autoethnographic stories of the companion book, written to re-establish "coherent self-narratives and [resolve] the incongruence between the reality of the loss and one's sense of meaning" (Neimeyer et al., 2010, p. 75).

My struggle to achieve reconciliation was evident, and these two theories are the building blocks on which I stood to make sense of a world without my father. The storytelling that precedes his death strives to bring meaning to what happened to him, while the narration post-loss attempts to relearn my world, myself, and my surrounding relationships (Attig, 2011). To come to terms with loss more deeply "requires that [we] identify, test, and recover trust in what remains viable, rather than define and appropriate new ways of being in the world" (Attig, 2011, p. 108). Consequently, before I could revisit my life's narratives, I needed to first meticulously scrutinize my cultural values and beliefs system as an Indian Christian.

References

Attig, T. (1991). The importance of conceiving of grief as an active process. *Death Studies*, 15(4), 385–393. https://doi.org/10.1080/07481189108252443

Attig, T. (2011). *How we grieve: Relearning the world* (Rev. ed). Oxford University Press.

Black, J., Belicki, K., Piro, R., & Hughes, H. (2020). Comforting versus distressing dreams of the deceased: Relations to grief, trauma, attachment, continuing bonds, and post-dream reactions. *OMEGA - Journal of Death and Dying*, 003022282090385. https://doi.org/10.1177/0030222820903850

Bonanno, G. A. (2009). *The other side of sadness: What the new science of bereavement tells us about life after loss.* Basic Books.

Calhoun, L. G., & Tedeschi, R. G. (2001). Posttraumatic growth: The positive lessons of loss. In R. A. Neimeyer (Ed.), *Meaning reconstruction and the experience of loss* [Kindle version]. Retrieved from Amazon.com.

Corr, C. A. (2015). Let's stop "staging" persons who are coping with loss. *Illness, Crisis & Loss*, 23(3), 226–241. https://doi.org/10.1177/1054137315585423

Devine, M. (2017). *It's ok that you're not ok: Meeting grief and loss in a culture that doesn't understand.* Sounds True.

Doidge, N. (2007). *The brain that changes itself: Stories of personal triumph from the frontiers of brain science.* Penguin Books.

Doka, K. J. (2016). *Grief is a journey: Finding your path through loss.* Atria Books.

Field, N. P., & Filanosky, C. (2009). Continuing bonds, risk factors for complicated grief, and adjustment to bereavement. *Death Studies*, 34(1), 1–29. https://doi.org/10.1080/07481180903372269

Frankl, V. E. (2006). *Man's search for meaning.* Beacon Press.

Freud, S. (1999). *The standard edition of the complete psychological works of Sigmund Freud* (Repr; J. Strachey, Ed.). Hogarth Press.

Jeffreys, J. S. (2011). *Helping grieving people: When tears are not enough: a handbook for care providers.* Routledge.

Klass, D., & Steffen, E. (Eds.). (2018). *Continuing bonds in bereavement: New directions for research and practice.* Routledge, Taylor & Francis Group.

Klass, D., Nickman, S. L., & Silverman, P. R. (1996). *Continuing bonds: New understandings of grief.* http://site.ebrary.com/id/10872589

Kübler-Ross, E. (1969). *On death and dying.* Macmillan.

Kübler-Ross, E., & Kessler, D. (2005). *On grief and grieving: Finding the meaning of grief through the five stages of loss.* Simon & Schuster.

LaGrand, L. E. (2001). *Gifts from the unknown: Using extraordinary experiences to cope with loss and change.* Authors Choice Press.

Lewis, C. S. (1961). *A grief observed.* Bantam Books.

Maté, G. (2012). *When the body says no: The cost of hidden stress.* Vintage Canada.

Neimeyer, R. A. (2001). *Meaning reconstruction & the experience of loss* [Kindle version]. Retrieved from Amazon.com.

Neimeyer, R. A., Burke, L. A., Mackay, M. M., & van Dyke Stringer, J. G. (2010). Grief therapy and the reconstruction of meaning: From principles to practice. *Journal of Contemporary Psychotherapy*, 40(2), 73–83. https://doi.org/10.1007/s10879-009-9135-3

Parkes, C. M. (1998). Traditional models and theories of grief. *Bereavement Care*, 17(2), 21–23. https://doi.

org/10.1080/02682629808657433

Parkes, C. M., & Prigerson, H. G. (2010). *Bereavement: Studies of grief in adult life, fourth edition.* Penguin Books.

Pennebaker, J. W. (2000). Telling stories: The health benefits of narrative. *Literature and Medicine, 19*(1), 3–18. https://doi.org/10.1353/lm.2000.0011

Shear, M.K. (2012). Grief and mourning gone awry: Pathway and course of complicated grief. *Dialogues in Clinical Neuroscience, 14*(2), 119–128. https://doi.org/10.31887/DCNS.2012.14.2/mshear

Stroebe, M., & Schut, H. (2010). The dual process model of coping with bereavement: A decade on. *OMEGA - Journal of Death and Dying, 61*(4), 273–289. https://doi.org/10.2190/OM.61.4.b

Taylor, S. (2015). *The calm center: Reflections and meditations for spiritual awakening.* New World Library.

Tolle, E. (1999). *The power of now: A guide to spiritual enlightenment.* New World Library.

Van der Kolk, B. (2014). *The body keeps the score.* Penguin Books.

Wolfelt, A. (2016). *When your soulmate dies: A guide to healing through heroic mourning.* Companion Press.

Worden, J.W. (2018). *Grief Counseling and grief therapy: A handbook for the mental health practitioner.* Springer Publishing Company, LLC.

Chapter 4

AN EASTERN PERSPECTIVE OF MOURNING

Examining Rituals and Religious Ceremonies of Indian Christians

Figure 2

A Map of Kerala

You cannot count on the physical proximity of someone you love, all the time. A seed that sprouts at the foot of its parent tree remains stunted until it is transplanted....Every human being, when the time comes, has to depart to seek his fulfillment in his own way.

—Maharishi Valmiki, *The Ramayana*

India is home to billions. In alignment with the reverence held for mothers in Indian culture, India is often affectionately referred to as *Bhārat Māta* (Mother India) or *Mā* (Mother) of her peoples (Gupta, 2001). Her colorful, at times painful, history paints the epitome of a resilient nation. A country that has endured the brutalities of colonization; and thus, conquered the throes of grief many times over. Growing up, my father instilled in me her wisdom, reciting a Sanskrit verse familiar to his home country: *Satyam, Shivam, Sundaram*. Loosely translated, the trilateral Indian philosophy exudes the significance of *truth*, *goodness*, and *beauty*. He taught me that these three principles governed the actions of humans who wished to lead a fulfilling life. And, as I entered the doctorate program to advance my knowledge as an educational leader, I was reminded of the importance of these virtues in the first textbook I opened: "Among the values that are believed to be *fundamentally human and transcendent* are goodness, truth, and beauty" (Murphy & Louis, 2018, p. 20).

I knew the work I had set out to do—to explore grief to its brutal core—was now a vocational calling, one my father approved. And, because of my cultural hybridity as an Indo-Canadian whose parents were born and brought up in Kerala, India, I had the additional benefit of experiencing grief culture through a second worldview lens. If I were to summarize my understanding of the eastern perspective of mourning, it would be that death is viewed through the lens of these three philosophical standards.

My father was a deeply religious man; hence, I knew the value he held for religious ceremonies and cultural rituals from all walks of life. Specifically, *his own*. When it came to the practices that correlated with observing a person's death, the "rites of transition conveying the soul from this world to the next" (Mosse, 1996, p. 465), he was prompt in handling the situation according to our longstanding Indian traditions. He believed death to be the occasion that calls us, as a community, to offer more than physical and emotional support, supplying mourners with spiritual sustenance. Often, he would assist with leading the community prayers that "focus on effectively separating the dead from the living" (Mosse, 1996, p. 465). Therefore, when he died, I devoted myself to participating in every established practice possible, ensuring that his soul left seamlessly and attained the eternal peace we believed awaited him. Traveling between India and Canada throughout the first year of my father's death, I engaged in year-long mourning traditions. And by learning how to braid eastern cultural rituals into my bereavement, I enhanced my ability to heal and honor a continuing bond with my father.

A Dual Approach to Mourning

As a family, we unwaveringly carried out both western and eastern mourning traditions. However, in Canada, once the funeral concluded, consistent community engagement faded alongside overt public expressions of mourning. Even though several external factors contributed to my prolonged grief, short-term western death rituals stifled me, leaving my internal processing incomplete. Bonanno (2009) states that "rituals are repeated because they are expected to have transformative powers" (p. 92); however, these traditions are not predominantly practiced in North America, leaving many grievers wanting. Klass and Steffen (2018) explain that "because of the decline of rituals, modern western societies are sometimes regarded as having insufficient therapeutic resources for grievers" (p. 214). Thus, grief authors have begun shedding more light on the healing power of these tasks by educating others on the need for increasing ritual literacy (Cacciatore, 2017; Doka, 2016). Weller (2015) supports, "ritual is a maintenance practice that offers us the means of tending wounds and sorrows, for offering gratitude, and for reconciling conflicts, thereby allowing our psyches regular periods of release and renewal" (p. 87). As in my case, the traditional services put in place immediately after my father's death laid a foundation for healing, but the abrupt mourning traditions left the ground bare and infertile. Castle and Phillips (2003) agree that:

Although the funeral facilitates the first phase of the grief process, it is unfortunate that in mainstream American culture, public expression of grief is not encouraged after this time, because the most difficult part of the grief process occurs after the funeral. (p. 44)

We are social beings who need to grieve communally, not as isolated individuals (Attig, 2019; Weller, 2015). Unlike collective grief, which is distributed and felt equally among all members experiencing the same tragedy, communal grief offers shelter, targeting and safeguarding a bereaved individual or family. To heal, I needed an outlet to harness and release my complicated emotions and bodily knowing of loss and death within a communal setting. Luckily, my dual upbringing rose to the occasion, filling in the western gaps of healing grief.

The eastern approach to mourning is active, shared, task-based, and ritualistic. *Ritual* can be described as "a means of attuning ourselves with one another, to the land, and the invisible worlds of spirit" (Weller, 2015, p. 73), and defined as:

> Any activity—sacred or secular, public or private, formal or informal, traditional or newly created, scripted or improvised, communal or solitary, prescribed or self-designed, repeated or one-time only—that includes the symbolic expression of a combination of emotions, thoughts, and/or spiritual beliefs of the participant(s) and that has special meaning for the participant(s). (Castle & Phillips, 2003, p. 43)

The religious ceremonies undertaken during the designated mourning period are some of the most ancient eastern traditions that exist, evoking a sense of spiritual duty tied to the dignity of the deceased, concluding their life honorably, and guiding the mourner to transmute suffering into venerable action. Within the Indian perspective lies the inherent belief that all transitions must be carried out auspiciously— then only will the soul achieve true liberation, and then only will those left behind feel at peace. For us, "death is understood as a process, a passage, rather than a termination of existence" (Inbadas, 2017, p. 338). Thus, I wanted to fulfill my spiritual and religious duties as a daughter, bringing proper closure to my father's life (Inbadas, 2017; Laungani, 2001; Mosse, 1996). Accordingly, I infused Indian Christian rituals into my mourning process, which consisted of communal, cyclical prayers, disciplined fasting, sacred ceremonies, and charitable contributions. Although the purpose behind Indian traditions is not always explicit, Mishra (2019) assures that these rituals are not random, but instead "an outcome of complex interactions between ideas, thoughts, and disciplined body techniques deeply influenced by the cultural sphere…[and] have the purpose of binding the individuals in a group, and the society, together" (p. 401, 403). Ultimately, these rites and rituals did help me move through my bereavement more effectively, bringing forward a significant lightness with each prescribed act I performed.

Rituals are not only designed to bring peace to the deceased, but they are also responsible for guiding the living out of the dark, liminal spaces incurred through loss. Often, many unanswered questions arise in the bereaved person's mind as grievers stop to ponder the true nature of life after death (Tedeschi & Calhoun, 2006). As a result, these religious ceremonies act as a vessel, holding the space required to find spiritual solutions to these questions, enabling mourners to align their beliefs with their loved one's passing. With each ritual I participated in, I was asked to surrender to the outcome of my father's illness *over* and *over* again. Quickly, I learned that on the eastern side of the world, bereaved individuals cope with loss by applying two balms: continuing bonds through ongoing rituals that liberate and memorialize the deceased, and communal grieving.

The Land of Sacred Rites and Rituals

I lift my eyes to the mountains—

where does my help come from?

My help comes from the Lord,

the Maker of heaven and earth.

—Psalm 121:1–2, *New International Version*

Because of its lush greenery and magnificent natural beauty, including its backwaters, rivers, canals, palm-lined beaches, and the Western Ghats—Kerala, which means *land of coconut trees*, is often referred to as *God's Own Country*. It is a southern state of India that rests on the tropical Malabar Coast, lining the Arabian Sea; the dominant spoken language is Malayalam. The population, close to 35 million, holds the highest literacy rate in the country at 96% (*Press Trust of India*, 2020).

The Malayalee peoples have a rich, distinct culture that follows traditions rooted in the bold religious history and geographic positioning of the state. My parents are native Keralites who lived in India until they were approximately 30 years old when they shifted to Canada.

Whenever I travel to Kerala, the aspect I take the most pride in is the visible, mutual respect shared among the citizens of multiple religions who live together amicably, side-by-side. As history has shown, this is not the norm for varying religious groups to coexist peacefully throughout all states in India. Yet, in his book, *A Place Within: Rediscovering India*, Vassanji (2009) describes the religious position of Kerala as follows: "The population is divided between Hindus, Muslims, and Christians; one is taken with pride to the city centre, where a mosque, a temple, and a church stand facing each other" (p. 23). Even though each religion follows different customs and traditions when performing rituals, the influence on one another's beliefs is apparent. When reading through the examples of ritual ceremonies described throughout this chapter, discernible differences from western Christian practices are evident, which may be attributed to the influence of Hinduism on Christianity in India (Mosse, 1996).

Although Hinduism is the religion of the majority in Kerala, Christianity dates back to the first century when Saint Thomas is said to have arrived in India and converted the people living along the Malabar Coast (Vassanji, 2009). My father was raised under the second-largest Christian denomination in India, the Church of South India (CSI), passed down from his father's side and was baptized under the Malankara Orthodox Syrian Church on his mother's side. In Canada, he was a practicing member of the Anglican faith and attended the same church in Calgary for close to 35 years. The interpretations of western and eastern cultural rituals presented throughout this chapter are based on these three denominations. In order to provide authentic and meaningful translations of Indian Christian rituals, most mourning traditions have been researched or translated by clergy, and some of the knowledge has been passed down from my family members and is thus, written in italics. Consequently, observances may slightly differ from one denomination to the next or transform from one family to the next. However, the ultimate reason for performing the ritual remains intact.

Western Traditions in Mourning

In Canada, Christians typically emphasize rites that need to be performed before the death occurs, and so my father's ritual journey began long before he died. Not knowing that he initiated the process himself, our priest later informed me that on the last Sunday he attended church, my father sought prayers, stating: *Something is wrong, but I don't know what.* He was hospitalized later that week. And, as he moved closer to his demise, our family took over. Multiple priests acknowledging both languages and cultures came to perform his last rites, signifying the cleansing of the soul, preparing for the passage from this world to the next. The reciting of holy words, affirming our values and beliefs, brought a sense of comfort, knowing he obtained ceremonious closure. After my father died, our immediate family members spent time with his body, but unlike in India, preparing the body for the funeral was left in the hands of professionals.

Canadian rituals post-loss centered around my father's funeral and consisted of making formal death announcements and planning the details of his final service. Since I took on most of these tasks myself, I felt I did align with previous studies that found "the organization of the period surrounding the funeral was important to process [the] loss" (Mitima-Verloop et al., 2019, p. 7). Narrowing down specific choices—photos, passages, poems, and hymn selections—that reflected my father's innate being was crucial to bringing him back to life a final time through the service. And with a sense of structure restored, a week later, a beautiful, traditional Anglican funeral was held in our family's church. People from all walks of my father's life, typically dressed in black attire, said their final farewells to their dear friend; the church was at maximum capacity, overflowing into the lobby and spilling into the upper hall. Those who attended stood in as pillars to resurrect us in our time of need, and this cushioned support was crucial, reinforcing that our loss mattered, which alleviated my grief. Kessler (2019) confirms that,

> Something profound happens when others see and hear and acknowledge our grief….The funeral ritual is important in witnessing grief because we will grieve alone for the rest of our lives. This is our last formal time to mourn together. (p. 45)

As I exited the chapel, trailing behind his casket, I looked for safe faces in the crowd to strengthen me—this is what mourners need, to feel safe in the face of great danger.

With a powerful ceremony that exuded my father's spirit, *Dad was felt in every corner of the church.* By summarizing and vocalizing what our father meant to us through our eulogies, my brother and I communicated our pride for him, bringing forward a sense of justice for his untimely death. Doka (2016) affirms, "the most effective funeral rituals are personal, highlighting the life and unique contributions of the person who died" (p. 227). After the service ended, he was laid to rest in a cemetery in Calgary, buried in the presence of our clergy and intimate circle. My mother, brother, and I each took a moment to reflect on his life and close his chapter. Then, the priest scattered dust across his casket, holy water sprinkled and blessed the burial grounds, and loved ones tossed in white roses as a last loving gesture. Truly, symbolizing the truth, goodness, and beauty of a life well-lived. Apart from planting a tree in my father's memory beside the grave a few months later, the prominent display of Canadian western mourning rituals ended. Yet, the true face of grief would only reveal its proper form once the funeral was over, expanding and swelling my suffering by the second, as "many bereaved people experience the most intense emotions between 3 and 24 months after the death" (Castle & Phillips, 2003, p. 44). Fortunately, my heart was adamant that my father left this world in the most honorable way possible, and two days after the funeral, I boarded a plane to Kerala to finalize his spiritual transition in his birthplace.

Eastern Traditions in Mourning

The night my father died, my mother came home and spread a white cloth, signifying my father's spiritual presence was still tied to the earth, overtop their bed. In India, an oil lamp would have been lit, bringing holy illumination to our darkness. However, in Canada, she kept an electronic light beside his bed instead. Symbolically guided by the Ascension of Christ, these items remain as is for the next 40 days until my father's spirit ascends. During this interval, no other person was permitted to sleep in my father's bed, nor were immediate family members allowed to eat meat, consume alcohol, undertake new ventures, indulge, or celebrate. Fasting observes that a prominent figure in the house—someone vital to our being—has died, initiating physical cleansing of the body during the mourning period, ensuring no additional toxins exacerbate one's grief. By engaging in this moral and spiritual act of service, we bond closer to God to uplift our well-being, and by purifying ourselves, we preserve the purity of our beloved's transitioning soul. My closeness with my father led me to fast and abstain from toxic or celebratory behavior for the remainder of the year—a commitment not always understood or honored within my social circles. But as per our customs, the year of mourning was for *mourning*, and I knew I had to make clean living choices to support my unbearable grief. Choosing not to numb my pain was a wise decision on my part; I worked through the raw and visceral complexion of my grief with persistence. I knew that any action that took focus from my wounds would only prolong my pain further—and so, my fasting was disciplined and religious.

In the final weeks of my father's life, he was never left alone in the hospital. For me, the cultural aspects of caregiving had become ritualistic, cathartic. Members of our community were to come and pay their last respects before he died. And on the first evening of his death, a prayer was organized in the deceased person's home. When one family member was taken from us, the rest of our community stepped in to offer prompt multidimensional support, as "the responses of others who are members of the bereaved person's spiritual or religious group(s) may have particularly strong influence on the outcome of the process" (Tedeschi & Calhoun, 2006, p. 109). Until this point in my life, I usually passively participated in the traditional prayers our parents enforced. Yet, here, with a house full of guests singing and praying for my father's soul, I awoke to the reverence of the unknown. *Where is my father now?* Weller (2015) details that "ritual is the pitch through which the personal and collective voices of our longing and creativity are extended to the unseen dimensions of life, beyond our conscious minds and into the realms of nature and spirit" (p. 76). The prayers, intonations, vibrations, sounds, songs, and chanting of the gathered company reassured us that his spirit was safe in the hands of God, simultaneously shielding us from the initial devastation and shock that accompanies death: "Beliefs and rituals, which provide an explanation for death and social support for the expression of grief, should reduce the confusion felt by the newly bereaved and might even be of psychological value in helping them to express their grief"

(Parkes & Prigerson, 2010, p. 210).

In India, this practice of prayer through communal worship, known as *Aradhana*, would continue for my father for the next seven days (until his burial). Kerala Christians hold symbolic prayers of mourning for the deceased on the following spiritual markers: the seventh day, *as Joseph observed a period of mourning for his father Jacob* (Genesis 50:10), the thirtieth day, *as Israelites mourned both Aaron and Moses* (Numbers 20:29; Deuteronomy 34:8), the fortieth day, *marking the ascension of Christ* (Acts 1:3–9), and the first death anniversary. In Canada, we gathered as a community on the first day, the fortieth day, and the first anniversary; the remainder of the prayers were observed by immediate family members only. At the family's discretion, yearly communal prayers can mark the death anniversary and remember deceased loved ones, a common practice in India.

If the death had occurred in India, the body would have returned to our house, as it must travel directly from the home of the departed to the holy burial grounds with the other family members (Laungani, 2001). The deceased's close relatives would gather to wash the body and clothe the family member in pure, white garments; married women are adorned in their white wedding sari and *minnu mala*, the traditional necklace tied on the bride by the groom at the time of marriage. A funeral cortège assembles as the community, also dressed in white, walks alongside the casket, singing intentional Christian hymns for the entire length of the final journey. *We believe the soul reaches its final destination on the voices of its loved ones.* Mosse (1996) describes how "the procession from the house to the cemetery involves crossing symbolic boundaries between the dead and the living" (p. 465).

Since my father passed away in Canada, the body arrived at the church separate from us, evoking a strangeness. Once we reached the chapel, my mother, brother, and I were the first to see him, and interacting with his cold body froze me, causing my emotions to be more neutral than I would have expected. We held a short intimate service in Malayalam for our close family and friends before opening the viewing to the public. Culturally, women covered their heads in front of the body, and all people made a sign of the cross, both gestures out of respect for my father's transitioning spirit—a reminder that holy acts were taking place. When the viewing concluded, the priest held out her hands and recited a blessing, we gave him a last kiss, and my brother, the eldest son, stepped forward to perform a final Indian Christian ritual. Before sealing the casket, he covered our father's face with a white cloth—ensuring his dignity was preserved, emphasizing the purity of his transitioning soul, and marking him with an emblem for the second coming of Christ. After he performed this religious duty, the traditional Canadian funeral began.

Once my obligations in Canada ended, I traveled back to the house where my father grew up. Over the long, two-day journey, sitting on a plane, alone and grieving, the realness of his death struck me. A tsunami of grief washed over me. But when I arrived in India, something shifted. *My father's presence surrounded me*, so prominent there, that I could not believe it myself. At times, I felt him running through the corridors or sitting in my grandfather's chair on the porch. Other times, I saw him contained in the natural beauty around me, such as the white butterflies fluttering about. His presence was so strong that I began rituals of continuing bonds with him immediately (Klass & Steffen, 2018). The ability to perform these acts while feeling my father's spirit boldly brought forward a sense of relief. However, as per our beliefs, *the soul remains close to its loved ones over the length of the first forty days*. Perhaps being in India for this interval of time amplified my feelings, but surely, after the fortieth day passed, the intensity of his presence also faded.

Because of the abrupt death of my father, chaos broke apart my meaning of life, leaving me with little direction on how to proceed. However, Mishra (2019) explains that the purpose of performing rituals is to "know what is to be done; the Right thing to do, the Right way to do that, and how to choose the Right course of action in conflicting situations by applying reason" (p. 410). Thus, the customary, longstanding traditions that were already in place before my father died brought a regimented structure to close his life using rituals I knew he held in high regard and considered right for him: "rituals also reflect the shared values and mythos of the community" (Weller, 2015, p. 77). Hence, once I entered my grandfather's home, I was advised on what needed to be done before returning to Canada.

The seventh-day prayer, symbolizing the burial of my father, was postponed until I arrived. On this day, my extended family and the surrounding community members initiated the road to recovery by gathering to pray and reminisce about my father's life, and these "traditions establish[ed] points of recognition and honor, boosting morale and instilling pride" (LaGrand, 2001, p. 156). I was asked to speak about my father and did so in his native tongue. Here, I understood the difference between summarizing his life in my first language and the mystical experience of articulating who he was in *his*. The sounds and vibrations of Malayalam rolled off my tongue, piercing a new layer of my grief. Without warning, the secondary loss of never hearing my father speak to me in Malayalam again crept up and surprised me, causing me to break. Ritual, in this sense, forced me to pay attention to the fine details of his loss. Concluding the prayer, I collected my emotions, rose to my feet, and gifted my father's church with devotional items in honor of him. Once this charitable ceremony was over, those who attended were fed a vegetarian meal, acknowledging our gratitude while adhering to our fasting customs as a community.

Our mourning rituals are rooted in charitable contributions, representing the humility we carry during the bereavement period. Laungani (2001) confirms that "it is a duty to engage in acts of piety and charity so as to ensure the peaceful repose of the departed soul" (p. 95). Acts of service, performed in honor of my father, *must enhance the lives of those less fortunate than us*. Throughout my trip, I made financial contributions to a variety of causes that were connected to my father's passions, *donating through his name*, not mine. I fed the residents of an orphanage, *ensuring I sat down and ate with them*. I purchased groceries for a struggling family, *delivering them with my own hand*. Almsgiving then was not only about how the contributions were given but equally to do with how they were received. As Weller (2015) notes, "there is something about ritual that resonates deep in the bone...relying not so much on speech as on gestures, rhythms, movements, and emotion...ritual addresses something far more primal than language" (p. 75). The intentional gesture of being of service to others continues every year on the anniversary of his loss.

Most of the rituals were communal, but some were private, solely connecting my father to me. Each morning, wrapped in his shawl, clutching his picture to my chest, I sat on my grandfather's chair and watched the sunrise, soaking in the restorative sights and sounds that awoke with the dawning light. It was a meditative experience, one that felt like I had direct access to the level of consciousness where he resided now. As Castle and Phillips (2003) support, "the goal of ritual is to transform experience by creating a bridge or connection between the concrete and symbolic, between the conscious and unconscious… between the world of the living and that of the dead" (p. 45). This was *my* time with my father—a time to be still and reflect on his death. A time to mourn freely, allowing my tears to flow without the interruption of others. Sometimes, I would sit pensively; other times, I would process the pain through my writing. Every day, without fail, I mourned this way. And this routine was a powerful therapeutic ritual, one that I formed independently: "the urge to create rituals to help us hold the intensity of day-to-day living exists deep within our psychic structure" (Weller, 2015, p. 76). I practiced this act of intentional crying in a structured and repetitive way every morning for all three trips to India over the next two years. This is how I released my pain by bringing attention to my concentrated suffering, embedding it into a solid routine, and then releasing my sorrow.

A second instance was when my uncle and I traveled to a famous church in Kerala, a spiritual landmark known for its healing power. Here, I lit four candles, one for each of my family members, symbolically representing that, spiritually, *we remain as one*. Kneeling, I prayed for repentance to remove the irrational guilt embedded within my grief. My tears overflowed with the *should have, would have, could have* scenarios beyond my control. Until now, my attempt to alleviate grief's amplified remorse on my own was unsuccessful. But, as LaGrand (2001) explains, "rituals and traditions free the mourner to think about life and the practical matters of living again" (p. 156). Perhaps visiting the church freed up a spiritual space for those thoughts and tears to release because, in the end, the sacred healing sanctuary relieved my pain as promised. Moore (2004) supports that "any method of dislodging the pieces of your life for reflection, is like baptismal water…clearing away the debris allows life to flow, with all the grace of beginning" (p. 62). Because of my travels through India, I felt a significant amount of the accumulating debris of grief had washed away, a release I would not have been able to bring forward on my own. The ritualistic nature of healing one's grief provided spiritual insight into my understanding of the metaphysical components of life, in time for me to return home and close the 40-day cycle of my father's death.

The evening of the *fortieth day* after he died, a community prayer was once again held in our home. Multiple priests led a small service in Malayalam, singing selected hymns, reading Bible passages that marked the spiritual milestone, and reciting holy prayers to help the bereaved assimilate their loved one's death—all the while burning frankincense throughout our home. Incense is a purification tool commonly used in Indian Christian holy ceremonies, adopted by Jewish practices, as interpreted from the Bible in the Old Testament and the book of *Psalms*: "Let my prayer be set forth before thee as incense; *and* the lifting up of my hands *as* the evening sacrifice" (*King James Bible*, 1769/2020, Psalm 141:2). Wafting frankincense in harmony with our religious prayers signifies that *the words of the faithful ascend upwards to heaven.* For me, the sounds, vibrations, and chanting instilled comfort; the imagery of rising incense provided a transformational visual; and the repetition of holy words and phrases brought a sense of ceremonious closure. Klass and Steffen (2018) describe these experiences as, "the involvement of the senses, through its ability to stimulate the imagination, is a further respect in which rituals contribute to distinctively experiential forms of cognition" (p. 221). To conclude, a meal organized by the community is shared before attendees leave, representing once more the communal bond during sorrowing times.

That night, after the prayer ended and the attendees left, my mother, my best friend, and I folded the white sheet on my father's bed and placed it under his pillow. I am not sure how to describe what came over me, but through the physical act of folding the sheet and putting it away, I felt a sense of release through bodily knowing (Klass & Steffen, 2018), a liberation. Doka (2016) corroborates my experience, explaining that rituals "are a powerful therapeutic tool—validating grief and allowing opportunities for catharsis" (p. 237). It would be the first time in 40 days that my grief gave a notable sigh of relief, and it would be the first time since my father died that—*I felt I could let him leave.*

Indian Christian prayers of mourning occur in three places: the home, the church, and the cemetery. Thus, our community gathered two more times that year. Once to bless the headstone and burial grounds after the monument was raised and once more in prayer to mark the first anniversary of his death, honoring his memory and supporting the family leaving their first year of bereavement.

A Community that Grieves Together

The stars were out and shining brightly when we returned, lonely and desolate.

—Jawaharlal Nehru, *An Autobiography*

Most families in India are tight-knit, with multiple families sharing the same house or living close to one another. All nearby residents make up the larger community, acting as extended families who share common spaces and, throughout the day, drop in without warning. As already evidenced in this chapter, the community comes together and provides stability for survivors in times of distress—sheltering bereavement. In Kerala, it is not the grieving family who arranges the funeral, final procession, and prayers for the deceased, but those in the community around them. The bereaved family is fully protected as they need time to process their loss, steering clear from decision-making unless direct input is required or stated. Van der Kolk (2014) supports that "for our physiology to calm down, heal, and grow we need a visceral feeling of safety" (p. 81); a reinforced sense of belonging is vital. This type of visible social support is crucial during the preliminary stages of grief as disbelief, shock, and denial are at the forefront of one's mind, and "the absence of such support among religious individuals may indicate heightened vulnerability" (Stelzer et al., 2020, p. 74). Mourners who perceive a secure social support system are less likely to experience ongoing complications or side effects from bereavement or identify as an at-risk bereaved individual who exhibits or participates in toxic behaviors (Rando, 1993).

When my father's health deteriorated, we were blessed to have a healthy body of people who supported all four of us. Immediately after he died, the community banded together to console our broken family, assisting with the funeral arrangements, organizing the necessary prayers, and ensuring that an abundant supply of food was in our home. However, after the heroic phase of mourning subsided, the social support slowly—*if not all at once*—diminished. The long-term care and deeper conversations that accompany death were not initiated, and our family was left to grieve in private because this was what was assumed to be needed. Yet, as Weller (2015) argues, "grief has *never* been private; it has always been communal. Subconsciously, we are awaiting the presence of others, before we can feel safe enough to drop to our knees on the holy ground of sorrow" (p. 74). But the proximity and open-home culture of India was unable to relocate here. And, living alone, island-confined, I specifically yearned for a stronger support system.

Unfortunately, second-generation Canadians' parents are often the only link to a more intimate cultural circle: "loss of a member of our families or communities can be represented by the effective removal of the web that represents the life of the deceased from the web of webs that represents these broader social contexts" (Attig, 2011, p. 153). Thus, my ties to the Malayalee community in Calgary somewhat severed after my father's death, and this was a secondary loss I was not anticipating. In Canada, most people seemed to avoid the topic of his death, or at times, *avoid me*, as texts and phone calls went deafening silent. Thankfully, I was able to lean on another homeland community.

By traveling to India and spending more time with my blood relatives, my bond with a community whose principal foundation was all about *community* strengthened. The relationships I formed in Kerala continued even after I returned home to Calgary and became my main source of comfort throughout my bereavement: "bringing our grief into the shelter of close friends and a vibrant ritual community is essential" (Weller, 2015, p. 89). No matter how many times I picked up the phone and called my relatives, *they answered*. No matter how many times I cried over losing my dad, *they listened and consoled me*. A timeline deemed acceptable and appropriate for mourning was not mentioned, and their response toward my grief was always the same: *You have to talk about it until you do not need to talk about it anymore. You have to cry about it until you do not feel like crying anymore.* In my darkest hour, they not only lit a lamp—they encircled me, preventing the light from leaving. In my most difficult time, their love resuscitated me because "we are not meant to be islands of grief...we heal as a tribe" (Kessler, 2019, p. 47). The nourishment offered by my relatives was not only cherished but actively flourished my healing.

Communal grieving means that community members approach another's loss with persistent empathy, fully witnessing the whole shape of their grief, feeling the loss deeply within and outwardly expressing this, and supporting the suffering of the mourner for as long as they need. As Attig (2019) notes, "when loss takes your breath away and suffering absorbs your energy, you depend on others giving to you....Only later, as your soul and spirit revive, are you able to give back to others" (p. 52). Now, when I must witness and stay present with the life-altering loss of another, I am fully prepared to offer the valuable gift of community in their time of need.

The support system in Kerala reminded me of Wohlleben's (2016) discovery in *The Hidden Life of Trees*. When stumbling upon the stump of a felled tree, he noticed "the surrounding beeches were pumping sugar to the stump to keep it alive...nutrient exchange and helping neighbors in times of need is the rule" (p. 2, 3). Communal grieving in India is like this; when a tree falls, a sophisticated network of inter-connectedness works together to keep the roots alive.

The Healing Nature of Rituals

Rituals soothe our raw wounds by offering physical movement to repair our spiritual brokenness and release our mind's suffering. For me, they reinforced a sense of belonging through communal grieving, brought a rightful conclusion to my father's death, and promoted spiritual solutions to come to terms with an undiagnosed illness through repetitious sensory experiences—all of which contributed to my recovery.

In India, a basic need to grieve among others was met. By evoking a sustained witnessing of my profound loss for an extended period, my extreme reactions and responses to grief were given room to settle. And since the space provided to process my prolonged emotions was in a communal setting, my grief reconciled safely. Even now, these rituals continue to honor my father's death through special announcements printed in the church bulletin every year, a regular practice within the Indian community. And each time I organize the details, select a new picture, and write a small reflection—my father's memory lives on. By maintaining these community practices, we are reminded not only of his death but that he once lived.

The sudden onset of an unknown illness left me feeling as though my father's story was incomplete. However, a rightful conclusion to his life emerged through the numerous sacred acts I performed. Essentially, I became more connected with the mysterious parts of life by interpreting the unknown and aligning it with our fundamental values and beliefs. I embodied the knowledge that the religious requirements of his spiritual transition had been met—that I had fulfilled my obligations and unwaveringly performed final acts of service for my father. Eventually, I realized that our eastern rituals were not only about supporting his transition but equally securing my successful passage into an afterlife of living post-loss.

Because I was unprepared for my father's death, many metaphysical questions and circumstances of perceived unfinished business arose. Since "rituals are *liminal* – they exist between the conscious and unconscious, affecting us in deeply emotional ways" (Doka, 2016, p. 226), a sacred space opened for me to seek and engage with spiritual solutions through prescribed bodily movement and sensory experiences. Whether I was participating in existing or self-made rituals, I consciously focused my attention inward, spotlighting heavy emotions, and permitting them to release through intentional actions. Castle and Phillips (2003) support that,

> Because of their out-of-the-ordinary feeling, rituals may help the bereaved to be less analytical and be more in touch with their feelings or even become aware of feelings that they were not conscious of before the ritual. As these feelings come to the surface, the bereaved person may feel a sense of release or catharsis, which is an important part of the grief process. (p. 49)

Thus, writing out my pain through an obituary or burning a candle to relieve my guilt allowed my mind to surrender to events that were beyond my control. Ritualistic ceremonies, such as making contributions with my hands or folding a white cloth allowed my spiritual pain to transform into something tangible, and by translating my suffering into human action, I found a way to *let it go*. By embodying my father's loss one sense at a time, my resistance to his death slowly evolved into acceptance.

When I reflect on the nature of prolonged grief from a place of intimate knowledge, I know that it is chaotic, disruptive energy that stirs restlessly and hopelessly within the griever. It has no place to go and no one to turn to—the griever, themselves, cannot make sense of it. The root cause of this form of anguish yearns to be felt, embraced, and released but has limited ways to do so. From my lived experience with prolonged grief, I believe, had I not consistently engaged with ongoing rituals to help process my pain, my suffering would not have subsided in the three years that it did. Apart from gaining mental clarity, I genuinely felt *lighter*, as the physical heaviness from complicated mourning was nurtured and then dismantled, without numbing, avoiding, or detracting from the pain. My joy for living resumed authentically because I allowed my suffering to exist in the same way.

My experiences throughout this chapter are not shared to dictate how rituals should be performed, but instead, they are meant to inspire those grieving who feel a cultural void in their current context. I hope that mourners seek out their own, perhaps buried, cultural traditions or create new avenues of healing that align with their values and beliefs system. In Indian homes, pictures of deceased family members are proudly displayed, adorned with flowers and incense, and typically have a lightbulb or candle lighting the image. Hence, rituals do not have to be extravagant acts to be therapeutic. They can be small traditions that instill pride in the griever, holding the death of their loved one sacred.

As we begin to overcome the large-scale challenges of COVID-19, we must consciously guide, counsel, and encourage the bereaved to create and fulfill meaningful long-term ritual practices, as an increase in prolonged mourning may be one of the many detrimental repercussions of a global pandemic. Without persistent action, "wounds close too soon, remain infected and never heal" (Weller, 2015, p. 17). And grief is not a thing to be cured—it is very much a sorrow to be healed.

Part I Summary: My Pilgrimage Through Prolonged Grief

There are no goodbyes for us. Wherever you are, you will always be in my heart.

—Mahatma Gandhi

Part I of this book provided a critical examination of past and present grief literature that has shaped our understanding of the phenomenon of grief. As depicted throughout the literature review, grief is not merely the emotional loss that most people assume it to be, instead bereavement "is one of the most painful occurrences in life" (Shear, 2015, p. 153) that affects our whole system as human beings. Measured against my one specific encounter with loss, certain cultural notions were either validated or deemed inaccurate. Alongside my reactions and responses to my father's death, I discussed the impact of various grief theories and models on my prolonged grief. The process models that actively pursued grief work, encouraged continuing a bond with my father, emphasized relearning my identity and reconstructing meaning, and did not enforce a timeline were the most helpful to me. Grief theories structured in this way also support grievers by educating non-grievers on the essentials of moving through grief effectively.

Last, I gave an overview of an eastern perspective of mourning as viewed through my ancestral roots in India, creating awareness around the powerful effect of ongoing death rituals on bereavement. By navigating through the two cultures I was raised with, I determined which assumptions negatively influenced my grief and which practices positively contributed to my healing. Initially, the western lens demonstrated solid communal support.

However, shortly after the funeral passed, my grief was placed in a contained box and labeled with expectations that did not match my experience, limiting my ability to work through and process the pain. By contrast, the eastern lens gave my grief the gift of community and room to breathe, addressing the metaphysical aspects of loss using ritualistic ceremonies. But, at times, the spiritual obligations overshadowed feeling through my suffering by heavily emphasizing religious duties. Being a member of both cultures enabled me to exercise more choice in my healing, taking the best of both worlds and applying it to my recovery: "Resilient souls find sustenance in familiar surroundings, draw from roots in family, community, history, and tradition; care and love deeply; and find grounding in the great scheme of things" (Attig, 2011, p. 1). Because of my extreme closeness with my father and my high level of attachment to him, the exploration of grief discussed in Part I is valid, credible, and relevant to future studies.

References

Attig, T. (2011). *How we grieve: Relearning the world* (Rev. ed). Oxford University Press.

Attig, T. (2019). *Catching your breath in grief: -- And grace will lead you home.* Breath of Life Publishing.

Bonanno, G. A. (2009). *The other side of sadness: What the new science of bereavement tells us about life after loss.* Basic Books.

Cacciatore, J. (2017). *Bearing the unbearable: Love, loss, and the heartbreaking path of grief.* Wisdom Publications.

Castle, J., & Phillips, W. L. (2003b). Grief rituals: Aspects that facilitate adjustment to bereavement. *Journal of Loss and Trauma, 8*(1), 41–71. https://doi.org/10.1080/15325020305876

Doka, K. J. (2016). *Grief is a journey: Finding your path through loss.* Atria Books.

Gupta, C. (2001). The Icon of Mother in Late Colonial North India: 'Bharat Mata', 'Matri Bhasha' and 'Gau Mata'. *Economic and Political Weekly, 36*(45), 4291–4299. Retrieved July 18, 2021, from http://www.jstor.org/stable/4411354

Inbadas, H. (2017). The philosophical and cultural situatedness of spirituality at the end of life in India. *Indian*

Journal of Palliative Care, 23(3), 338. https://doi.org/10.4103/IJPC.IJPC_61_17

Kessler, D. (2019). *Finding meaning: The sixth stage of grief* (First Scribner hardcover edition). Scribner.

King James Bible. (2020) King James Bible Online. https://www.kingjamesbibleonline.org (Original work published 1769).

Klass, D., & Steffen, E. (Eds.). (2018). *Continuing bonds in bereavement: New directions for research and practice.* Routledge, Taylor & Francis Group.

LaGrand, L. E. (2001). *Gifts from the unknown: Using extraordinary experiences to cope with loss and change.* Authors Choice Press.

Laungani, D. P. (2001). Hindu deaths in India—Part 1. *International Journal of Health Promotion and Education, 39*(3), 88–96. https://doi.org/10.1080/14635240.2001.10806179

Mishra, A. (2019). *Hinduism: Ritual, Reason and Beyond.* StoryMirror Infotech Pvt. Ltd.

Mitima-Verloop, H. B., Mooren, T. T. M., & Boelen, P. A. (2019). Facilitating grief: An exploration of the function of funerals and rituals in relation to grief reactions. *Death Studies*, 1–11. https://doi.org/10.1080/07481187.2019.1686090

Moore, T. (2004). *Dark nights of the soul: A guide to finding your way through life's ordeals.* Gotham Books.

Mosse, D. (1996). South Indian Christians, purity/impurity, and the caste system: Death ritual in a Tamil Roman Catholic community. *The Journal of the Royal Anthropological Institute, 2*(3), 461. https://doi.org/10.2307/3034898

Murphy, J., & Louis, K. S. (2018). *Positive school leadership: Building capacity and strengthening relationships.* Teachers College Press.

Parkes, C. M., & Prigerson, H. G. (2010). *Bereavement: Studies of grief in adult life, fourth edition.* Penguin Books.

Press Trust of India. (2020, September 8). *International Literacy Day 2020: Kerala most literate state in India, check rank-wise list.* Hindustan Times. https://www.hindustantimes.com/education/international-literacy-day-2020-kerala-most-literate-state-in-india-check-rank-wise-list/story-IodNVGgy5hc7PjEXUBKnIO.html

Rando, T. (1993). *Treatment of Complicated Mourning.* Research Press.

Shear, M. K. (2015). Complicated grief. *New England Journal of Medicine, 372*(2), 153–160. https://doi.org/10.1056/NEJMcp1315618

Stelzer, E.-M., Palitsky, R., Hernandez, E. N., Ramirez, E. G., & O'Connor, M.-F. (2020). The role of personal and communal religiosity in the context of bereavement. Journal of Prevention & Intervention in the Community, 48(1), 64–80. https://doi.org/10.1080/10852352.2019.1617523

Tedeschi, R. G., & Calhoun, L. G. (2006). Time of change? The spiritual challenges of bereavement and loss. *OMEGA - Journal of Death and Dying, 53*(1), 105–116. https://doi.org/10.2190/7MBU-UFV9-6TJ6-DP83

Van der Kolk, B. (2014). *The body keeps the score.* Penguin Books.

Vassanji, M. G. (2009). *A place within: Rediscovering India.* Anchor Canada.

Weller, F. (2015). *The wild edge of sorrow: Rituals of renewal and the sacred work of grief.* North Atlantic Books.

Wohlleben, P., & Billinghurst, J. (2016). *The hidden life of trees: What they feel, how they communicate: discoveries from a secret world.* Greystone Books.

Part II

Showing

Chapter 5

THE REVELATIONS OF EAPEN

Deconstructing my Autoethnography

The purpose of my autoethnographic study was to use storytelling to intimately explore the phenomenon of grief while investigating the benefit of expressive writing on bereavement. The 41 stories presented in the companion book—*The Revelations of Eapen*—were written to evoke emotion in the reader by showing the impact of loss and will be of use to anyone who wishes to understand grief more deeply. However, these self-narratives will be most beneficial for those who are grieving. Due to our lack of death education, we heal grief by finding relatability in one another's experiences. And even though I narrate my own story of loss, I have carefully crafted each vignette to encompass the widespread sufferings of the grieving community. These stories will be difficult to read, as they will cause the griever to pause, reflect, go back, confront, process, and alleviate deep pain. But I assure mourners, in the end, the deep-seated pain of grief will find alleviation.

Using the art of storytelling, my narration as the protagonist was weaved through the raw events of my father's death, examining the cultural exchanges that transpired. These revelations uncover the hidden layers of grief, bare the chaotic and distressing change in family dynamics, unveil the repercussions of a culture consumed by grief illiteracy, and support the powerful potential of the Continuing Bonds model (Klass & Steffen, 2018). Apart from the trials and tribulations, I account for the subtle spiritual interplay that occurred throughout my father's loss—divine sparks that softly spun in the background of his death and continued to guide me afterward. Although the stories themselves are published separately, this chapter aims to deconstruct my autoethnographic process, laying out the building blocks for educators, researchers, and grievers who wish to engage with evocative storytelling to support bereavement.

The Foundation of Storytelling

Grief is a constructed experience that can be influenced by the closeness of the relationship with the deceased (or lack thereof), circumstances of death, family background, personality, medical history, mental health history, resiliency patterns, previous experiences with loss, and the social support systems available post-loss (Attig, 2004; Bowlby, 1998; Parkes & Prigerson, 2010; Rando, 1993; Shear, 2015; Wolfelt, 2003). Thus, my epistemological stance as a researcher exploring the phenomenon of grief embraced the constructivist lens which states, "that all knowledge, and therefore all meaningful reality as such, is contingent upon human practices, being constructed in and out of interaction between human beings and their world, and developed and transmitted within an essentially social context" (Crotty, 1998, p. 42).

The foundation of using storytelling as a method of research drew from the qualitative research design that is "pragmatic, interpretive, and grounded in people's lived experiences" and "typically enacted in naturalistic settings, focuse[d] on context, and is emergent and evolving" (Bloomberg & Volpe, 2016, p. 44). The stories were written using evocative autoethnography (Bochner & Ellis, 2016), which allows for the embodiment of emotional, compelling responses to arise in readers by using "thick description, a value of aesthetics, evocative and vulnerable stories with little concern about objectivity and researcher neutrality" (Le Roux, 2017, p. 199). I wanted to narrate the multi-layered depth of death, grief, and grieving, adding authentic insights and knowledge that would benefit both academia and the grieving community. Hence, the research setting, data collection methods, and organization processes were critical factors when recreating my story of loss accurately and with validity.

A Setting for Writing

Consistently, I wrote all 41 stories in my home office. Besides having a quiet and meditative feel, it is also a safe space where my father knew I frequently wrote. His pictures, acting as an emblem of purpose, were in clear sight and provided meaningful inspiration whenever my creativity was stagnant. While my home office was where the writing took place, I used other settings and sites to trigger my memory and generate ideas, such as his spaces in our home, the hospital where he died, his burial site, his birth site, and the house where he grew up in India.

Collection of Memories

The primary method of data collection for this study stemmed from evoking personal memory "which taps into a wealth of information on self" that can be drawn out and "written down as textual data" (Chang, 2008, p. 72). To embody the vivid details of my father's final days, Bochner and Ellis (2016) suggested using two strategies: systematic sociological introspection and emotional recall. The first strategy challenges the writer to bring up "thoughts and feelings from a social standpoint" (p. 167), while the second strategy encourages the author to travel back into a scene through their imagination to spark "deeper emotional remembering" (p. 168).

Sociological Introspection

In my specific case, a response to grief that I encountered was severe memory loss. Retrieving information was difficult for me, and I relied on others to fill in the blanks of events as they occurred before and after his death. I started keeping track of the information I received to secure my father's story, fearing my failing memory would force him to slip away. In retrospect, as my prolonged grief and academic journey evolved, I realized I was writing extensive field notes for my study (Bochner & Ellis, 2016) so that I could engage in "interactive introspection" (Holman Jones et al., 2013, p. 98) effectively.

Field Notes. My field notes consisted of journal entries, letters to my dad, a *Grief Map* that identified and labeled my explosive emotions (refer to Chapter 7), and jotted notes of casual conversations with others who provided insight into my grief patterns. I gathered evidence over two years, and this strategy of recording individual and collective observations improved my ability to recall the moments I had blocked out. Thus, my field notes acted as self-observations and self-reflective data (Chang, 2008) that built the bones of these stories. Even though these documents did not transfer word-for-word into my writing, they supplied the narratives with rich insights. Rereading old journals, letters, and sketches written during the initial phase of loss, prompted an emotional response, which led to more accurate story writing. Therefore, these documents helped shape "an evocative tale that had the elements of a good story" (Bochner & Ellis, 2016, p. 171), further augmenting my ability to recall the subject matter.

Emotional Recall

When my father died, my emotional response was overwhelming. The slightest unnerving sensory perception (sight, sound, smell, taste, touch) would transport me back to the hospital, sitting beside him, watching him die. When I started writing the stories, I turned this revisitation into a storytelling strategy. If I read about another's experience with death, or saw a familiar critical scene on the television, or heard a song that reminded me of my father—I was triggering my emotional recall system. And when that happened, I wrote. Next, I systematically ordered this information, using objective data collection methods, such as chronicling, inventorying, and visualizing (Chang, 2008), to supplement and stimulate my memory recollection processes.

Chronicling the Past. Chang (2008) states, "in the data collection stage, chronicling is a useful strategy through which you give a sequential order to bits of information you collect from memory" (p. 72). Before I tested the waters with storytelling, I used date stamps of photos, videos, holidays, anniversaries, special occasions, text messages, events saved in my online calendar, and ongoing conversations to shape and sharpen the accuracy of my memory. Then, I marked these dates down in a personal planner to visualize the sequence of events, as I would write them in chronological order. Last, I placed these items on a "comprehensive autobiographical timeline" (Chang, 2008, p. 73), ranging from the first time I noticed my father's illness past his funeral. Here, I was selective and specific, ensuring to include the traumatic events and ordeals I had not yet processed.

Inventorying Self. Once the events were ordered, "inventorying" helped eliminate chaos and provide structure by connecting the self-narratives to themes and "rank[ing] them by importance" (Chang, 2008, p. 88). The overarching theme answered the question: *What is my experience with loss?* I needed to capture the emotional journey of my father's death by narrating the significant last memories I had with him. To be precise, the stories were separated into four key categories. The first three occurring pre-loss: *In the Beginning, In the Middle, In the End.* And a fourth pertaining to the trauma and secondary losses that materialized post-loss: *A Year of Firsts.* The last category focused on grief as it evolved through welcomed and unwelcomed social interactions.

Visualizing Self. As noted in Chapter 2, after my father's death, I experienced symptoms of Post-Traumatic Stress Disorder; scenes from the hospital or pivotal turning points (such as his extubation from life support) would spontaneously burst through my mind. These intrusive visuals were exceptionally strong during the actual timeline of events: November 21–January 14. Thus, I used this timeframe to my advantage: "Visualization strategies…intend to help stir your memories and organize loosened memory fragments" (Chang, 2008, p. 81). During these months in 2018 and 2019, when my PTSD heightened, I sat with the bombardment of images and used them as visualizing techniques to bring me back to the scene. This strategy, summoned alongside grief counseling, consciously sparked my emotional recall, transforming my memories into plots filled with descriptive, sensory details as they occurred in the past, bringing them into the present.

A second visualizing strategy I used was looking at physical pictures. Before my father was admitted to the hospital, when I first observed something was *off*—I took a series of photos of him on my cellphone, documenting his illness. Not only did these pictures help strengthen my memory, but they also evoked emotions in the reader as "a visual image can convey a message more efficiently and powerfully than a series of words" (Chang, 2008, p. 81). Gathering these images, I created an album chronicling his last days from October to January. The photos acted as date stamps and provocations for my writing, and they became a visual storyboard that helped me intentionally organize the data under the headings noted above. And since grief stories are trying to preserve the memory of deceased loved ones, the writer wants the exact image of the deceased to be present in the reader's mind, so including these photos in my data enhanced the therapeutic value of storytelling. As Chang (2008) supports, "visual data complement textual data and sometimes supersede the benefit of textual data because visual data make long-term impressions on viewers" (p. 109). I knew their focus would be on my father, and this relieved me. Hence, I encourage those crafting their own stories to include photos of their loved ones as they see fit.

Invoking Organization

Numbers were symbolic guides for me, often appearing out of thin air and providing subtle relief for the distressing symptoms of prolonged grief through gentle reassurance. When organizing the data, I used these numbers to infuse symbolism within the structure. Since my father passed away on January 14 (1/14) at 1:41 A.M., I chose to write 41 *Revelations*, organized under four headings, that used the number five (his birthday) and 14 (his day of death) throughout the telling of central details (ex: *the five keys of continuing bonds*). And since "the story is what gives artistic shape to autoethnography" (Bochner & Ellis, 2016, p. 82)—to effectively organize my writing—each vignette followed a specific plotline, coinciding with the title of the revelation.

As Bochner and Ellis (2016) explain,

> Often, an autoethnographer's story is a tale of two selves, a journey from 'who I was' (before my epiphany) to 'who I am' (now), after living through these events…in a good story, we often witness a main character transformed by a crisis. (p. 91)

The epiphany in these stories arose from my experience of severe, prolonged grief that comes face-to-face with cultural, grief illiteracy. Here, the protagonist (me) reaches an *aha!* moment (Denzin, 2014; Holman Jones et al., 2013) that more compassion, understanding, and innovative tools are required when dealing with grief and supporting the grieving community. My subsequent transformation is communicated through the stories written in the last section, dedicated to narrating my growing understanding of grief and grieving post-loss.

Ethically Sound Storytelling

Since autoethnography is a self-reflective study of one's engagement with and personal experience of a wider, cultural experience through examination and critique (Holman Jones et al., 2013)—it is often misunderstood as a methodology that cannot impose harm or cross established ethical boundaries. However, our stories as autoethnographers tell of the everyday social interactions with others (Bochner & Ellis, 2016), and thus, ethical considerations should be sound throughout one's writing process. To pen *The Revelations of Eapen*, I had to consider the ethical perspectives of my father, myself, my family members, and other minor characters factored into the plot of my stories, ensuring no harm toward myself or others arose from the data (Ellis, 2007).

My Father

The main subject explored throughout my data is my relationship with my father. The death of a loved one is a topic frequently explored autoethnographically, and according to Ellis (2007), "people lose some legal rules of privacy after they die…because they cannot suffer as a result of damaged reputations" (p. 14). Hence, my father's inclusion would be considered ethically sound.

Still, in my eyes, my father is a heroic figure, and my writing portrays him as such from start to finish. Moreover, one of the last phrases he spoke to me was: *You always know what I'm thinking*. Using this as a marker, I am inclined to stay true to the story he would want me to write, and grief storytellers should, when possible, make their best attempt to do the same. Lastly, on his death bed, my father requested me to write a book about the revelations made through him. Therefore, I know I am fulfilling his wishes.

Potential Risks or Benefits to Self

Writing through my encounter with grief has, at times, exacerbated my suffering. I have felt emotionally drained through the consistent and persistent examination of prolonged grief as I simultaneously experienced it. Initially, my continuous reading of grief literature caused anxiety, heaviness, and lethargy. Thus, I had to establish boundaries and strict self-care practices to support myself to complete this work and ensure my safety when executing storytelling.

If I was not in a good state of mind, I forwent writing that day. Or, if my PTSD swelled, I did not further antagonize myself by returning to those dark spaces of loss. Using my emotions as a compass was crucial to move through all 41 stories. Overall, the positive benefits of writing far outweighed the negative. Through storytelling, I noticed a gradual lessening of the unbearable weight of my sorrow. I saw a drastic reduction in the PTSD symptoms that consumed me daily. And, most importantly, writing through my shadowing grief cast a light on my suffering that had a clear, positive impact on my reconciliation with loss.

Relational Ethics

Although my self-narratives were written from my point of view, relational ethics reminds me that complex storylines always involve multiple characters, perspectives, and interactions that weave and intertwine together to create a profound plot. Therefore, "relational ethics recognizes and values mutual respect, dignity, and connectedness between researcher and researched, and between researchers and the communities in which they live and work" (Ellis, 2007, p. 4). In autoethnography, staying vulnerable is the strength of the process; however, a skilled autoethnographer should find ways to keep the study's authenticity intact, even when personal, intimate, or revealing details must be omitted due to the possibility of causing harm. Ellis's (2007) advice is to use the heart and mind to create storylines sensitive to the subjects involved.

To explore death and grief was uncomfortable and messy; the actions of others were under scrutiny, and more often than not, unpleasantries surfaced. When writing my data, I intentionally kept the names of hospitals, staff members, and other secondary characters anonymous. I ensured my critique of grief illiteracy brought the concerns of the larger grieving community forward instead of spotlighting issues solely based on me or my frustrations. Delicately, I weighed and measured the emotional reactions of others against the unfolding chaos of the stories and the lasting impression they should leave on the readers, keeping the aim of autoethnography in mind, which is to to highlight human suffering (Bochner & Ellis, 2016).

Because of the distress that challenges family dynamics during the death of a loved one, I had to navigate those turning points with high sensitivity, using carefully constructed language that stayed true to our actual experiences. With evocative writing, underlying truths can still materialize even if the corresponding interactions are modified (Ellis,

2007)—and so, I often stopped to ask myself, *is this telling necessary?* If the sequence brought a significant truth to light on the phenomenon of grief and the lasting impact loss leaves on a family, I kept writing. If it did not contribute to the research, I adjusted, modified, or eliminated the interaction.

Although the stories reveal my innermost feelings (and not necessarily the thoughts, feelings, or behaviors of my family and community members), "we often fear that those in our stories will be hurt by what we've revealed" (Ellis, 2007, p. 17). To counter this problem, I created a channel of open communication with my family members, seeking their advice, input, and approval for all 41 stories before publication. Also, a close friend of mine who was present in the hospital read over the stories as a second set of eyes to ensure that my emotions were not telling a biased tale or narrating an unfair representation of minor character interactions that emerged throughout his loss. Last, as I read through the data, it was evident that the culmination of each story took on a multiple perspective approach, clarifying the irrational actions of family members and bringing the focus back to my father. The understanding that his death provoked upsetting, emotional reactions in all of us was apparent.

Concluding Remarks of an Autoethnographer

In the past—*and still, present*—qualitative methods, such as storytelling, were deemed inferior or not considered credible research. For most of my academic career, qualitative research was labeled as the *easy way out*. Yet, my companion book, consisting of roughly two hundred pages of concrete and detailed writing, penetrated the innermost layers of the phenomenon of grief, with all 41 stories successfully aligning with Le Roux's (2017) criteria for evaluating autoethnographic rigor: *subjectivity, self-reflexivity, resonance, credibility*, and *contribution*. Because I was a single author, writing in a single setting, with one specific case of complicated grief that only "affects 2 to 3% of the population worldwide" (Shear, 2015, p. 154), I needed to ensure my data spoke to the common issues of limited grief etiquette and insufficient cultural mourning practices within modern North American societies. Therefore, *The Revelations of Eapen* was the most grueling, demanding, intensifying, and satisfying research I have conducted. By deconstructing my autoethnography in this chapter, my hope was not only to support future autoethnographers conducting similar studies but to shed light on the intricacies involved when creating accurate, reliable, and valid qualitative data. Alongside my eye-opening narration of death and grief, my autoethnographic stories thoroughly demonstrate that parts of us cannot be quantified in numbers. The core of who we are, as human beings, must be fleshed out using the deep and insightful art of storytelling.

References

Attig, T. (2004). Meanings of death seen through the lens of grieving. *Death Studies*, *28*(4), 341–360. https://doi.org/10.1080/07481180490432333

Bloomberg, L. D., & Volpe, M. (2016). *Completing your qualitative dissertation: A road map from beginning to end* (3rd ed). SAGE Publications.

Bochner, A. P., & Ellis, C. (2016). *Evocative autoethnography: Writing lives and telling stories*. Left Coast Press.

Bowlby, J., & Bowlby, J. (1998). *Loss: Sadness and depression*. Pimlico.

Chang, H. (2008). *Autoethnography as method*. Left Coast Press.

Crotty, M. (1998). *The foundations of social research: Meaning and perspective in the research process*. Sage Publications.

Denzin, N. K. (2014). *Interpretive autoethnography* (Second edition). SAGE.

Ellis, C. (2007). Telling secrets, revealing lives: Relational ethics in research with intimate others. *Qualitative Inquiry*, *13*(1), 3–29. https://doi.org/10.1177/1077800406294947

Holman Jones, S. L., Adams, T. E., & Ellis, C. (2013). *Handbook of autoethnography*. Left Coast Press, Inc.

Klass, D., & Steffen, E. (Eds.). (2018). *Continuing bonds in bereavement: New directions for research and practice*. Routledge, Taylor & Francis Group.

Le Roux, C. S. (2017). Exploring rigour in autoethnographic research. *International Journal of Social Research Methodology*, *20*(2), 195–207. https://doi.org/10.1080/13645579.2016.1140965

Parkes, C. M., & Prigerson, H. G. (2010). *Bereavement: Studies of grief in adult life, fourth edition*. Penguin Books.

Rando, T. (1993). *Treatment of Complicated Mourning*. Research Press.

Shear, M. K. (2015). Complicated grief. *New England Journal of Medicine*, *372*(2), 153–160. https://doi.org/10.1056/NEJMcp1315618

Wolfelt, A. (2003). *Understanding your grief: Ten essential touchstones for finding hope and healing your heart*. Companion Press.

Part III

Synthesizing

Chapter 6

THE IMPACT OF STORYTELLING ON BEREAVEMENT

An Analysis

Expressive writing has been the focus of several studies in the past, aiming to explore and analyze the therapeutic value of disclosure on human suffering. Using language to express, validate, and relieve one's emotional distress is not a new discovery; however, an ongoing debate exists as to why writing is effective. Most theories speculate that keeping emotional distress to ourselves or inhibiting disclosure avoids confronting trauma (Leopore & Smyth, 2002; Pennebaker & Beall, 1986). Pennebaker and Smyth (2016) argue that,

> Disclosing or confronting a trauma helps us understand and ultimately assimilate the event. By talking or writing about a secret experience, we are translating the event into language. Once it is language based, we can better understand the experience and ultimately put it behind us. (p. 11)

My father's death was not a secret. But the grief I endured—the physical, social, psychological, behavioral, and spiritual repercussions that arose because of it—was kept in the dark for most of my bereavement. Thus, my disclosure not only revolved around the painful memories our family encountered in the hospital, but my stories also brought awareness to the insensitive nature of grief illiteracy, a lingering societal darkness.

This chapter analyzes my evocative autoethnography, *The Revelations of Eapen*, to explore how storytelling that leaned on expressive writing helped me actively process and effectively move through my grief. My data consisted of 41 stories (revelations) that used first-person storytelling to disclose the cultural interactions that occurred before, during, and after my father's death while narrating the wildness of prolonged grief. By anatomizing these stories, I discuss the central themes that emerged from my writing using the narratives-under-analysis approach (Bochner & Ellis, 2016; Bochner & Riggs, 2014), providing a framework for therapeutic storytelling that targets bereavement.

Writing about these experiences brought the full scale of my loss forward, uncovering the *why* behind the acute nature of my grief. I found expressive writing highly beneficial in releasing my trauma, allowing me to consciously navigate through my father's death and the subsequent complicated grief that formed because of it, from my own point of view and in an uninterrupted fashion (Pennebaker & Smyth, 2016). Overall, studies have found that writing about a traumatic event in a meaningful way has positive benefits, such as improved mood and immune function; decreased stress and doctor visits; increased self-regulation and post-traumatic growth; and boosted motivation to seek re-employment, following the loss of a job (Leopore & Smyth, 2002; Pennebaker & Smyth, 2016). My experience matched those of previous participants, whereas initially, while writing, I became visibly upset, feeling an increased sensation of grief, *crying out every word on the page*. But after completing the self-narratives, and in the long term, I felt a stronger sense of purpose, resiliency, positive well-being, post-traumatic growth, and eventually, I even reunited with joy (Calhoun & Tedeschi, 2001; Pennebaker & Smyth, 2016). Through rigorous self-introspection and storytelling, my complicated grief became uncomplicated and lifted.

A few authors have targeted their discussions toward the effect of writing on grief. They have found that self-reflection, meaning-making, awakened and preserved memory, articulation, catharsis, changed perceptions, and tributes to the deceased have all created beneficial outcomes for the griever (Bostico & Thompson, 2005; Furnes & Dysvik, 2011; Neimeyer, 1999). Furnes and Dysvik (2011) summarize that "emotions are embedded in the body as impressions, and we experience them as expressions. The experience of grief creates an impression, and when this impression finds articulation, the person may achieve understanding" (p. 16). My analysis aims to add to the existing knowledge of cathartic writing, specifically its effect on prolonged grief, by discussing the themes, patterns, and categories that emerged from writing out a lengthy, detailed account of loss and deciphering how storytelling helped me reconcile my father's death.

Writing Through my Grief

My study was designed to address the effect of storytelling on bereavement after I encountered crippling, complicated grief. Often, engaging in verbal narratives was not enough because, for most of my bereavement, I was simply at a loss for words. Apart from trauma's impact on the functioning of my brain, other factors interfered with my recovery—psychologists and counselors were a timed endeavor; my family members were struggling with their grief, unable to fully support mine; and most of my friends were either indifferent or pushed my grief aside. I had to find a way to create a form of disclosure that was not bound by the limitations of others. The result was the creative task I undertook to plan and write the companion book, *The Revelations of Eapen*. Gordon (2000) supports that "through art forms man can…break the seal that locks [her] into [her] inner world" (p. 146). In my own time, and in my way, I released my suffering into the outer world using the narrative art of storytelling. But before I could move into translating my emotional experience into language, I first had to learn how losing my father had affected my brain.

The Effect of Trauma on the Brain

My grief was traumatic. For the first two years, my mind was so severely affected that I could not recall the full details of my father's loss nor remember the order of events that led to his demise. Because of this, I could not communicate the story sensibly to others, and this inhibition became an impediment to my healing. My thoughts and spoken language were frozen, repeating the same points of my father's death over and over again, without resolution. Pennebaker and Smyth (2016) explain that "the failure or inability to translate traumatic experiences into language has been implicated as one possible cause of PTSD…linking our emotional memories to language is often beneficial" (p. 145). Thus, bridging this gap was vital for me.

The ongoing frustration of losing verbal reasoning persuaded me to research the effect of trauma on the brain to find out what was happening to me on a biological level. I learned that my physical symptoms, as well as my reactions and responses to grief, aligned with someone who had gone through a severely traumatic event (Levine, 2015). The crushing blow of losing my father had shut down the left side of my brain, causing me to lose sequential order, linguistic ability, and logical reasoning (Van der Kolk, 2014)—all of which explained my abnormal behavior. Consequently, this prevented me from making clear connections to how things happened in chronological time. By furthering my understanding of how the traumatized brain functions, I learned why the story shattered and fragmented.

> Breakdown of the thalamus explains why trauma is primarily remembered not as a story, a narrative with a beginning, middle, and end, but as isolated sensory imprints: images, sounds, and physical sensations that are accompanied by intense emotions, usually terror and helplessness. (Van der Kolk, 2014, p. 70)

The marked events in the hospital became scattered and disorganized, creating a disconnection between my mind and the tragic plot that unfolded. A year after my father's death, bits and pieces of what happened suddenly resurfaced and scarred me, as forgotten memories rushed to the front of my mind, delivering both shock and confusion (Levine, 2015). According to Van der Kolk (2014), "people cannot put traumatic events behind until they are able to acknowledge what has happened and start to recognize the invisible demons they're struggling with" (p. 221). And these invisible demons—*stored memories*—tormented me.

Although on the outside I was quiet and meek and seemingly under control, on the inside, vivid scenes of him dying were terrorizing me: "to be traumatized is to be condemned to an endless nightmare, replaying these unbearable torments, as well as being prey to various obsessions and compulsions" (Levine, 2015, p. 8). Without my dad, my will to live was fading, and I knew internal repair was needed before a desire to form new experiences returned. *How does an introvert find solace?* Usually, they turn to a diary or journal to make sense of an event on paper, one that the mind cannot quite grasp. Pennebaker and Smyth (2016) support that "translating abstract thoughts and emotions associated with a traumatic event into written words with a linguistic structure may allow for the traumatic event to be better understood and integrated into one's understanding of 'self' and the world" (p. 146). Since I had used writing to heal through painful situations in the past, organically, I sought comfort from this tool to heal through the severity of my grief as well.

When the devastation of my father's demise struck me, our story was compromised. Essentially, I had to relearn the story of loss and unlearn my reliance on my dad, rewiring the neural networks that depended so heavily on him (Doidge, 2007). Writing was a tool that helped me rewrite my perceptions, connecting the dots of the outcome and deepening the language I needed to move beyond my suffering: "putting our deeply emotional experiences into language and words facilitates our brain's capacity to help us manage our emotional states" (Pennebaker & Smyth, 2016, p. 39). By writing these 41 stories, I reinforced neural pathways that reframed my perspective of the events in the hospital, encouraged meaning reconstruction in loss, restored and rebuilt my identity, and created a manuscript to relearn my place in the world (Attig, 2011; Neimeyer, 2001; Pennebaker, 2000).

My Writing Process

My father loved reading my writing. Working as a freelance writer for two years, Dad kept track of all of my articles and purchased every magazine I had written in, ensuring he gave me positive feedback for each one. It came as no surprise that before he died, he insisted I write a book. The title he left me with on his deathbed, *The Revelations of Eapen*, was the only starting point I had when I set out on this journey. From here, the central theme of writing revelations instead of standard chapters came forward. And operating under the structure of a repetitive theme *did* contribute to my relief (Pennebaker, 2000). Next, when my doctoral supervisor asked me how many self-narratives I envisioned writing, I gravitated toward *41*, bridging the connection to my father's time of death. In short, every aspect of my writing process tied directly back to my father. Not only did this motivate me to write to the end of all 41 stories, but a sense of keeping him alive through my writing emerged. Gordon (2000) posits that,

> Creative work in the arts in particular depends on the capacity to live—almost simultaneously—in two or even more realities, the internal and the external, the personal and the collective, the conscious and the unconscious; and it is in the creative arts that experience at the symbolic and experience at the pre-symbolic level may in fact coincide. (p. 147)

Because the subject matter is meaningful, traumatic, and sensitive to me, I had to ensure that solid guidelines were put in place, strengthening the purpose of my writing and eliminating the possibility of rumination, venting, and re-traumatization (Pennebaker & Smyth, 2016). As each story unfolded, I kept the suggestions made from previous expressive writing researchers in the back of my mind: write in a safe setting, limit writing increments, write over multiple sessions, take designated breaks, control the use of negative emotions, make positive emotions more pronounced, use poetic prose, change perspectives, search for benefit and insight, construct a coherent story, find your voice, and manifest the best future version of yourself (Pennebaker & Evans, 2014; Pennebaker & Smyth, 2016). Because of the guidance of these authors, my stories *safely* stirred healing within.

Narratives-Under-Analysis

I embarked on constructing self-narratives with the assumption in mind that if I wrote out the story of my loss in full detailed disclosure and stood back, meaningful correlations would jump off the page (Bochner & Riggs, 2014)—and they did. I moved forward with analyzing my autoethnography using the narratives-under-analysis approach. Bochner and Ellis (2016) state,

> In narratives-under-analysis we treat stories as 'data' and we analyze them to arrive at themes, types, or storylines that hold across stories…we see ourselves as scientists representing reality in order to develop theory and reach generalizations…we reduce the story to content and then analyze it, hoping to find larger categories, themes, or patterns. (p. 185–186).

When I removed myself as the main character and looked at the writing through a scientific lens, performing an "uninterrupted reading of the data" (Holman Jones et al., 2013, p. 116), a greater appreciation for storytelling arose, specifically around its capacity to support grief work. The categories I had identified in my analysis emerged twofold: *the art of storytelling* and *the four cornerstones of grief stories*. The themes under the first category spoke specifically to the writing—the structure, language, drafting, and revision of a story. While the patterns from the second category specifically delved into the writer's grief—relationship building, designing a blueprint of grief, strengthening spiritual health, and leaving a lasting footprint. Both of these categories had a positive impact on my recovery.

The Art of Storytelling

Before loss, storytelling played a vital role in how I made sense of the world—as a student, as a teacher, and as an Indo-Canadian. Thus, when I could not make sense of my father's death, I turned to narrative writing: "Storytelling is the means by which we represent our experiences to ourselves and to others; it is how we communicate and make sense of our lives; it is how we fill our lives with meaning" (Bochner & Riggs, 2014, p. 197). Post-loss, all meaning had vanished as the structure of my life was broken, and the story I once knew to be true fell apart, shattering my identity. Over time, I became frustrated with my prolonged grief, and when distress is evident, research tells us that we must consciously make an effort to navigate the internal chaos using "self-awareness...becoming aware of our *inner* experience and learning to befriend what is going on inside ourselves" (Van der Kolk, 2014, p. 208). Storytelling then became a way to reacquaint myself with who I was before my dad died, rebuild who I became after he died, and reinvent who I needed to be without him.

The construction of a coherent story produced positive health outcomes for participants in previous writing research studies. Smyth et al. (2001) concluded that "the organization aspects of narrative play a critical role in the health benefits of writing about traumatic events and that written disclosure lacking narrative formation may not be beneficial" (p. 171). Because I felt like my father's death and the severity of my grief fell through the cracks, storytelling provided me with an outlet to openly express my trauma (Pennebaker, 2000), reconstruct a world of meaning (Neimeyer, 2001), and solidified that the memory of our story was both preserved and heard (Furnes & Dysvik, 2011). In short, storytelling secured a stage for my grief to stand on and heal.

The Structure of a Story

The structure of my writing was relevant because "*having* a coherent story to explain a painful experience was not necessarily as useful as *constructing* a coherent story" (Pennebaker, 2011, p. 11). Evocative autoethnography gave me a platform to design stories that would stir emotion in both the reader and writer (Bochner & Ellis, 2016), bringing my grief to life so that I could label and release it. Gordon (2000) deems this desire to manifest "essential…making and creating is what I have called the 'urge to incarnate', or to 'make flesh'" (p. 142). And by doing so, the invisible veil that safeguarded my grief from the public lowered. Hence, my openness to disclose my complicated grief to society—to my family, friends, strangers, and even at times, my-self—mattered. This was the foundation upon which the stories were structured, vulnerability.

With the help of the emotional recall tools discussed in Chapter 5 (Bochner & Ellis, 2016), I used pictures, timestamps, and field notes of conversations with others to successfully chronicle the past (Chang, 2008), creating a succinct timeline of the events. This information was then organized under four chronological headings: *In the Beginning*, *In the Middle*, *In the End*, and *A Year of Firsts*. Once I achieved restored order, I used the narrative elements of Freytag's Pyramid (1863) to reconstruct the story: exposition, rising action, climax, falling action, and resolution. By ordering the events as they occurred and plugging them into a plot diagram, I began searching through my memory and remembering more of what happened instead of incessantly sifting through the fragments I chose to remember. Slowly, the seemingly minute details that had fallen to the wayside resurfaced, and a clearer, more complete picture formed. These critical factors I had forgotten, and thus not taken into account, built a story of loss that I *could* reconcile with. The self-reflective space and the intentional structure of the stories opened up an avenue for remembering deeply, which then encouraged my healing.

The Language of a Story

The language I used to tell my story, *my father's story*, provided a pivotal turning point in my reconciliation. I had to ensure that every detail belonged where I put it, as "deliberate construction of details for use in stories can be a positive experience in bereavement" (Bostico & Thompson, 2005, p. 13). The writing was no longer about simply bringing my interactions to light. It was *how* I wrote about them that impacted my grief, thus "the shift [wa]s thinking *with* language to thinking *about* language" (Olson, 2016, p. 242).

Often, my grief had taken over the wording, creating emotional exaggerations that were not necessary. On multiple occasions, I had to reexamine the language I was using (*Dad was the only person in the world who cared about me*) and replace it with more accurate syntax (*Dad was one of the few people in my life who showed me he cared*). Grief was amplifying my emotional state to all-or-nothing type scenarios, creating Dad-or-nothing type dialogue. By reframing my mindset to remind myself that my mother equally cares about me, I ended up catching a lot of these overcompensations created by the pain of his loss. And, when I caught myself revising a statement once, more instances arose. Soon, it became apparent that I was intentionally crafting language that: considered family pronouns and transparency, balanced emotions, made use of poetic prose, and weaved my parents' authentic tongue directly into the text.

Family Pronouns and Transparency

In his book, *The Secret Life of Pronouns*, Pennebaker (2011) states,

> The writings of those whose health improved showed a high rate of the use of I-words on one occasion and then high rates of the use of other pronouns on the next occasion, and then switching back and forth in subsequent writings. In other words, healthy people say something about their own thoughts and feelings in one instance and then explore what is happening with other people before writing about themselves again. (p. 13)

During the rereading of each story, I began to notice that I frequently wrote "my father" instead of *our* father in narratives that included both me and my brother; or I wrote "my pain/my loss/my grief" in family stories that should have indicated *our* pain, *our* loss, *our* grief. By revising my use of personal pronouns, I allowed the walls of my grief to come down, reminding myself that his loss is our collective loss, a suffering we share as a unit. These adjustments strengthened my awareness of their grief, simultaneously increasing my compassion and empathy toward my mother and brother, as bereavement had tricked me into feeling as though I was walking through this misery alone. Because of this, a reparative benefit that mended our broken family dynamic was a natural and unexpected outcome of storytelling. Frequently, I stepped back and asked myself, *Is this what actually happened? Or is this your grief? Was their grief the driving force behind their actions?* I had to reassess and reframe our interactions through the lens of loss to ensure the language I was using was accurate to our

125

circumstances. It was equally important to be honest with my behavioral responses to grief, discussing the sour aspects of the story where I was not my ideal self. A case in point was when I irrationally argued with my mother:

> *I do not remember why the conversation took a drastic turn; I only remember that it did. Honestly, at this point, I doubt anything that she could have said or done would have been right—I was insistent on making mountains out of molehills. Before I knew it, I blew up in the middle of the hospital room.* (Revelation 9)

The closer I moved toward an accurate, honest, and transparent portrayal of conflict, the more I trained my mind to settle, and the more likely writing became an effective component of healing.

Balancing Emotions—60/40

Although Pennebaker and Evans (2014) suggest using negative emotions in moderation, I found that when constructing a grief story, I had to spill the intense, unbearable emotions onto the page to achieve true catharsis. And the more I wrote, the more I wanted to keep going, as "man's need to communicate and validate this inner world, is probably one of the most powerful incentives that drives man to make art" (Gordon, 2000, p. 146). However, keeping the expressive writing guidelines in mind, I consciously tried to match the negative emotions, words, and phrases with positive ones. For instance, in Revelation 2, I wrote: *This night would later solidify into one of those remorseful memories that taunt the griever*—and later neutralized this statement with—*However, purpose is always in the eye of the beholder…the regret of leaving him that one night, forced me to stay glued to his side every night thereafter.* In this way, I was not avoiding the hard-to-digest emotions, actions, and aspects of loss that needed to find a release. Instead, I supported my grief by bringing attention to the hidden, revelatory facets that coincided with the tougher ones.

Another crucial component of storytelling was to express the joyful or humorous moments that shone through during his hospitalization, to memorialize the good alongside the bad. An example of this arose through my father's laughter, while entrenched in his delusions: *When I heard his contagious chuckle bubble and boil over, I could not help but join in and shake with laughter also. In the dark room, a light* (Revelation 16). By humanizing the experience and bringing the lighter issues forward, *a glimmer of gratitude rose from my grief* (Revelation 39). By the end, I estimated the stories balanced nicely at a 60/40 split—the larger portion allowing me to release the heavy, negative emotions of death and grief.

The Poetry of Grief

The next aspect of language that proved to be beneficial to my recovery was using poetic prose throughout the retelling of my story because "grief by its nature is poetical, elegiac" (Cacciatore, 2017, p. 44). Surviving the death of a loved one is a journey that travels beyond common language; so, to connect more deeply with my emotions, I had to draw them out using poetic devices. Gordon (2000) explains that,

> When one discusses percepts and imagery one really discusses mental contents, the furniture of the mind, as it were…because a symbol interlinks psychic functions and different levels of experiencing, it has innumerable meanings and can never be totally reduced or 'translated'.…For, where a symbol operates, there is always meaning-behind-meaning-behind-meaning. (p. 109–110)

Often, I did not want my grief to be totally understood; my father's death was too painful to restrain or constrain into what was deemed normal suffering, defined in literal terms. A driving factor behind creating these stories was to let grief out of the *socially acceptable box* (Revelation 38) we try to place it in. Thus, purposefully and intentionally, I wove symbolism, imagery, metaphors, similes, hyperboles, alliterations, assonances, ironies, clichés, idioms, puns, personifications, juxtapositions, and allusions into the writing to interact with my grief. I wanted the words to reach out and into the reader, permitting them to feel the ache of my loss directly.

Specific literary devices were more comforting to create than others, namely: clichés, idioms, allusions, assonances, and alliterations. The poetic beat that flowed with the latter two always steadied and stilled me, bringing a balanced rhythm back to my racing heart—and so these techniques dispersed throughout the stories. Like others, I struggled with constructing the language of grief, a concept not formulated in our culture. The limited vocabulary I did have encouraged the use of clichés, which later, I went back and revised. But the initial writing of commonly used or overused phrases reduced my feelings of isolation by reintroducing familiar speech; it felt as though a small return to society was possible. Similarly, by including idioms my father used to say—*making mountains out of molehills, let the cat out of the bag, the straw that broke the camel's back*—a sense of him returned also. And, by alluding to some of my father's favorite songs, books, and movies, figurative language further embedded his personality into the stories. By channeling an interplay of words, I released my suffering in a way that would not have occurred using everyday dialogue. As Neimeyer (1999) supports, "sometimes literal words fail us in conveying our unique sense of loss…to move beyond the constraints of public speech, we need to use words in a more personal way, and draw on terms that are rich in resonance and imagery" (p. 78).

Lastly, I noticed how specific metaphors made their way into my writing more than once: *a light in the darkness, crossing a threshold,* and *being born again.* Essentially, poetic prose validated the intensity of my grief and carried me into a new state of being. The rich descriptions found in my writing acted as a vehicle to put an inexpressible loss into words, without fearing judgment, and with the assurance that the reader would not be able to debate the agony of my pain. Finding a way to translate the inexpressible into the expressible, figurative language helped me communicate and process my father's death more effectively.

Weaving Authentic Tongues

While drafting, I decided it was essential to embed my parents' mother tongue, Malayalam, directly into the prose. As a second-generation Canadian, the secondary loss of my parents' Indian dialect, the language they raised me with, was devastating to witness slowly fade and vanish alongside them. To combat this, I weaved their common vernacular and key phrases into the dialogue, securing a way to preserve this vital aspect of my upbringing. As I read and sounded out the Malayalam words on the page, I evoked nostalgia, a sensation of hearing my father speak to me personally arose. The stories acknowledged the words my father said to me, *the way he said them.* Thus, weaving authentic language healed me by keeping the feeling of my father alive in this context.

Drafting a Story

By the end of my writing process, I had written out three separate drafts. The first draft consisted of only a dozen vignettes outlining the most traumatic parts of my father's death, equating to the *standard* approach to expressive writing, disclosing the "deepest thoughts and feelings about a stressful or traumatic event" (Pennebaker & Smyth, 2016, p. 163). The second draft elaborated on and added to the existing content, expanding the vignettes into 41 self-narratives. This version now included *cognitive processing*, shedding light on my "thoughts and feelings in an attempt to derive more understanding and insight"; *exposure*, reexamining my "deepest thoughts and emotions about the same event"; and, *benefit-finding*, used to "identify an event and then focus on the positive aspect of the experience" (Pennebaker & Smyth, 2016, p. 163). Although the weight of my grief had noticeably lessened after writing out the second draft, something was lacking—something in my heart still felt amiss.

I began researching and reading more deeply into the purpose of autoethnography, seeking a resolution to my problem. I expanded my understanding of what great storytelling entails and how evoking emotion in the reader is enhanced by inviting them into the most intimate areas of the author's life. I realized I had not given the reader the full scope of my relationship with my father; I had only opened a door into his final moments. On a whim, I revamped and rewrote all 41 revelations once more, only this time, I included short, vivid memories of our close father–daughter bond over my 31 years spent with him. With this third draft, the self-narratives transformed into short stories, producing a version that felt whole. The inclusion of these fond memories turned out to be the most challenging and heartbreaking pieces to write.

When I thought I had cried out all of my pain in the second draft, without warning, these flashbacks with my father brought forward a fresh abundance of tears, cleansing me of my sorrow once more. Not only were these short pieces emotion-evoking, but they were also a pivotal turning point in my reconciliation with loss, reminding me why my agony was relevant and real. By sifting through my most cherished memories with my dad and writing them down on paper, I reached into the core of my suffering and pulled out the foundational aspects of loss. Grief was not constructed from a single, culminating event—the affliction formed over time, taking in every moment I spent with him. Now, I surrendered to the severity of my grief, fully accepting my reactions and responses to his loss as well-warranted. This gave me the confidence to take a stand against the grief-illiterate actions of others, as the doubt they planted regarding the importance of my loss was squashed. The cleansing and purging delivered through writing this final draft added a critical layer of meaning to my story, finally loosening the firm grip of grief: "In some way, suffering ceases to be suffering at the moment the hurt finds a meaning" (Frankl, 2006, p. 113). As a constructivist researcher, I successfully constructed the whole story by *redrafting*. Now, I felt complete; now, the reader would understand and empathize with my pain; and now, I could let it go.

Revising a Story

"Rewriting is the essence of writing" (Zinsser, 2006, p. 4)—and I, wrote and rewrote and rewrote and *rewrote*. Revisions became essential to my telling of "a more organized, honest, and coherent story" (Pennebaker & Evans, 2014, p. 73). The more I edited, examined, and revised my ideas, the closer I felt I was to releasing the painful details of my father's loss. And the more I engaged with my reworkings and revisions, the more previously irretrievable information resurfaced. Suddenly, memories of incidents that occurred in the hospital would surge forwards, nudging me to add details that would make the story more whole. Schank (1990) explains that "human memory is a cluster of experiences, each labeled in complex ways. These labels allow for the retrieval of relevant experiences at the right time so that we have a story to tell" (p. 23).

On more than one occasion, I shared these new recollections with my best friend, who, two years after Dad's death, exclaimed, *You never told me that before*. Two years later, prompted by my writing, I began remembering: "Traumatized people have their lives arrested until they are somehow able to process these intrusions, assimilate them, and then finally form coherent narratives that help put these memories to rest" (Levine, 2015, p. 8). And because this only started happening more frequently after I began aggressively editing the stories, I attribute the occurrence to my complete immersion into the writing process. Through my rigorous revisions, my memory was triggered, strengthened, and restored, allowing me to tell a full version of the story.

Revising the stories was also helpful because, as Pennebaker and Evans (2014) point out, "you can remake your own history with the benefit of hindsight...extensive editing and rewriting of your story helps you focus on what is most relevant to your life right now" (p. 73). By reading, rereading, and annotating the content, I made stronger connections to the benefit-finding moments that bloomed through the cracks of loss. And, when analyzing the data, I found that I sprinkled the phrases—*in hindsight, reflecting on, looking back now*—on numerous occasions throughout most of the stories, and these deliberate realizations carried therapeutic value (Pennebaker & Smyth, 2016). Without intentionally looking for areas of improvement, the beneficial insights of loss may not have evolved, nor would I have traveled deeper, exposing the suffering held in my subconscious mind:

> *The last fall is that moment, the conclusive evidence my subconscious needed to rationalize what it was seeking all along, a need to take responsibility for my father's death. Examining my innermost thoughts and unmasked guilt only revealed the raw nature of my distractibility—a belief I held firmly in my heart for all of these years—the impression that, truly, he is going to be okay because he is going to live forever.* (Revelation 2)

Although ongoing debate exists as to whether or not editing holds therapeutic value (Pennebaker & Evans, 2014), when writing grief stories, I believe the answer depends on how deeply a person wants to heal or how much grief work they are willing to engage. I found that constructing a concise sentence matters since "a sentence is a well-defined unit of written language" (Olson, 2016, p. 117). I could *feel* the sentences on the page, and if the delivery was off, the sentence needed to be revised, and when it was revised, my emotions felt heard. And not only did the sentences need to feel right, but the paragraphs needed to visually appeal to my senses. Often, I found myself trimming unnecessary information because the block paragraphs needed to align a certain way, gliding the emotions across to the reader using a more impactful tone. Because of this need for symmetry, the exaggerations of grief were often edited out, eliminating the possibility of tainting my father's story with false perceptions, ensuring conciseness was intact.

With each draft, I evoked emotion, and with each revision, I re-evoked emotion, providing a cathartic release that emptied my tears. The more I edited, reworked, rewrote, and retold the story of my father's loss, the better I felt. Hence, not only did aggressive editing help me process my emotions more effectively, but it also encouraged me to form new connections with the material, allowing me to identify what truly mattered in my narration, permitting me to discard the likely overcompensations of my grief. This careful process of *revising* enlightened my perceptions, the nature of my disclosure, and the integrity of my story. As Olson (2016) supports, when we edit a piece of writing, we bring awareness to our own ideas:

> The metalinguistic concept of a sentence brings these underlying structures into consciousness as objects with particular properties such as *clear* or *ambiguous*, *grammatical* or *ungrammatical* and, importantly, as *implied* or *entailed*. Such inferences are justified by appeal to wording rather than to belief. (p. 116)

Finally, when the revisions were complete, and the story was told the way I needed to tell it, my grief no longer lived stifled inside of me. Instead, it was released into the world in the form of a beautifully written masterpiece on loss, waiting to connect with others.

The Four Cornerstones of Storytelling

Narrative writing was directly tied to my ability to recover and reconcile with my father's death; I did find release through storytelling my disclosure. However, by placing my narratives under analysis, I quickly noted that grief stories differed. To effectively heal through the loss of my father, the storyline had to go beyond the plot diagram. Thus, four cornerstones of storytelling emerged and secured my writing: *relationship building, designing a blueprint of grief, strengthening spiritual health*, and *leaving a lasting footprint*. Pennebaker and Evans (2014) reiterate that "merely having a story to explain a trauma does not predict health improvement…the person must build or construct a story over the course of writing" (p. 49). And noticing that these four cornerstones consistently embedded themselves into all 41 stories was crucial to understanding why writing helped me move through my grief.

Relationship Building

Because I conducted an autoethnographic study, examining the social interactions that mingled with my grief and exploring my relationship with other characters were vital aspects of each story. However, it was not until I began writing out the data that I started to acknowledge the therapeutic value hidden in relationship building, a term I use to describe a new level of character development. Through this cornerstone, I paused each scenario and tried to determine the root cause of another person's actions by contemplating their motives and switching perspectives with them (Pennebaker & Evans, 2014). Moreover, when constructing grief stories, I had to expand this expressive writing guideline one step further and interpret their behavior against the experience of death and loss—*what were their reactions and responses to grief?* As I brought their true intentions forward, my mind was able to release the hurt, confusion, and resentment I felt toward them, simultaneously easing my grief: "making sense and finding benefits from one's experience of loss are both associated with decreased complications in grieving" (Holland et al., 2006, p. 183). Reframing my perceptions to understand the perspectives of others during a tragic event supplied me with probable explanations that alleviated the uncertain aspects of my suffering. And once I successfully saw the event from their point of view, I strengthened my relationship with them through my writing, extending my hand through words. By exploring my mindset, as well as grasping the mindset of my father, my family members, and the grieving community, my painful feelings shifted to empathy. Using empathy to build relations with other characters allowed me to repair past conflicts in real time.

Understanding Myself

Grief led me to believe that I had not done enough for my father in his final days, and the regret and remorse that stemmed from this false notion fueled a fire that lit my suffering ablaze. But as I developed our relationship more deeply in writing, I strengthened my perception of our interactions over the past 31 years. My words painted a vivid, more accurate picture of the beauty of our bond. Suddenly, the things I knew in my heart to be true were visibly laid out on the pages in front of me, bringing a peace of mind that I did perform my daughterly duties—I did everything in my power to save him, to keep him comfortable, to honor him. I went above and beyond, not only in his final days but over the course of our time together. The irrational guilt that accompanied *my mind, muddled with mourning* (Revelation 39), was wiped clean. And gathering proof of the complete portrayal of our father–daughter relationship substituted an enormous amount of gratitude in place of my grief: "When bereaved people can experience being grateful for the lives of their deceased loved ones and the impact the lives of the deceased made on others, they are better able to accept the death" (Tyson, 2013, p. 335). Attig (2011) emphasizes the importance of relearning one's identity after loss, but here, I learned that *reshaping* my past identity, erased by my grief, was equally important. By building a stronger relationship with myself, I witnessed my evolution occur. My naïveté before my father's loss transformed into a higher calling to educate others on the impact of grief, "that is why man is even ready to suffer, on the condition, to be sure, that [her] suffering has a meaning" (Frankl, 2006, p. 113). Post-loss, I valued life more, I tightened my relationships, and I empathized more easily with others, wanting to support their suffering:

> Benefit-finding refers to the significance of the loss and entails the survivor's paradoxical ability to uncover a "silver lining" in the personal or social consequences of the loss, such as enhanced empathy, reordered life priorities, or a closer connection to other people within or beyond the family. (Holland et al., 2006, 176)

Within the *aha!* moments of the stories, I enhanced my self-understanding by eliminating self-doubt, increasing my confidence in my abilities, and establishing a purposeful mission to help others through my writing.

The second aspect of relationship-building with myself arose through a marked increase in the value I held for my culture and religion. Before storytelling, I knew a commitment to both aspects existed, but I had not emphasized their importance on who I was. As I researched and interviewed family members, rigorously digging out the *why* behind our way of life, a surprising amount of information organically floated to the surface. The cultural impact my parents had on my sense of self became more evident, and rich knowledge about our family's heritage was pulled from within. All at once, my understanding of family increased immeasurably. I understood more deeply that our traditions and customs were important to me and my healing, and this sense of pride was separate from my obligatory duties. Alongside my loss, a spiritual community arose and sheltered me from the fatal blow of losing my father, as if my ancestors were present, guiding me down the path of reconciliation. The stories then became a way of expressing this inward and outward understanding of loss, educating others on the Indian-Christian way of grieving, preserving my culture at the same time. A divide was removed between me and the audience, and I no longer had to justify my Indian rites and rituals for mourning. They were laid bare for everyone to read, bridging a gap between me and my surrounding society.

Understanding my Father

The storyline between me and my father, my primary parent, solidified my attachment to him, explaining the intensity of my grief. However, an underlying reason for my complicated mourning was that I felt his death was too sudden, taking us by surprise and taking from him the time needed to come to terms with his death. However, when I stepped into my father's shoes and wrote from his perspective, I found several clues that alluded to his awareness around his impending death and the actions he took before he died came alive:

> *Later, in India, my uncle elaborated on their conversation, how the two of them talked for over an hour, as Dad asked his younger brother question after question. Eventually, when my uncle inquired into the intention behind his interrogation, my father responded: I think this will be our last conversation. We won't get another chance to talk after this. As his words crashed down on my ears, my mind went blank. The constant swirl of thoughts, forming my reasonings and imaginings of the untimely nature of his death, were brought to an abrupt halt. Only two words managed to survive my shock—he knew.* (Revelation 6)

Within the stories, I delved into the foreshadowing scenarios I had learned from outside sources, information I had gathered after he died. Then, I used these details to build a version of the story that was not visible to me. On multiple occasions, I used the words *he knew* or referred to instances where *he initiated the journey himself*—to support the growing evidence that my father understood he was dying. Although I was struggling and lagging, he was of sound mind and knew nothing was untimely about his death. And the more I wrote about these unspoken revelations, the more I asked myself, *if he was at peace with his death, why can't I be?* Looking through my father's lenses, knowing he left the way he wanted to, I finally surrendered to the natural cycle of life that everyone wanted me so badly to accept. By repeating the phrase, *he mattered,* throughout the last section of the stories, I reinforced the meaning of his life after he died. The realizations I made along the way eased my ability to build a new relationship with my father by continuing bonds with him.

Understanding my Family Members

The death of a loved one caused our family dynamics to erode and explode, leaving the remaining three of us devastated (Bonanno, 2009). The emotional push and pull of our grief simultaneously pushed and pulled each of us in separate directions, and because I am more like my father, my struggle to connect with my mother and brother exacerbated my grief. Yet, storytelling allowed me to examine loss differently, delving into my mother and brother's perspectives. Consciously, I tried to place myself in their roles and imagine the loss of a husband, *Undoubtedly, for most of their lives, they only had each other* (Revelation 5); and, my brother's father, *Listening to his playlist, it registered that he too knew Dad well. That, they had spent five years together, without me* (Revelation 28). Once again, I was able to reconstruct the story I was holding onto and reconcile hurtful actions and interactions that I could not comprehend at the time by using perspective-shifting techniques. Because "only with time are we able to begin to appreciate what others were thinking, feeling, and seeing during the same period" (Pennebaker & Evans, 2014, p. 49).

With my mother, I was able to retrace my steps and see how losing my father created a sensation of anger that was unfairly directed toward her. I was able to come to terms with the irrational behavior that moved through me as a defense mechanism: *As crystal-clear as it is now, at the time, I could not see how anticipatory grief moved through my body. That, I regressed to childlike mannerisms to cope with the loss of my primary parent* (Revelation 9). With my brother, I was able to resolve conflicts that consistently arose throughout our dad's hospitalization. A prime example of this was my brother's decision to put off taking a photo with our father in front of the Christmas tree. At the time, his choice did not make sense to me, and as my father became more ill, it created festering resentment. But as I wrote through the issue, a different interpretation emerged, one that I had not considered before:

> Each family member did the best we could with the knowledge and information we had during those final months, not knowing they were his final months. My brother's part was not to come down for a few minutes and take a picture. His part was putting in the endless hours of work to raise and decorate the tree in the first place. I realized had it not been for him, Dad's aha! moment to take advantage of a golden opportunity for his family would not have materialized. I would not have had one last merry Christmas memory with my dad. (Revelation 6)

When I looked at the situation from a different angle, a fresh outlook emerged, allowing my hurt to be integrated and forgotten (Pennebaker, 2000). It also dawned on me that if this moment ate away at me, it was most likely destroying my brother. Pennebaker and Evans (2014) state that "a guiding principle of transactional writing is to become conscious of another's perspective, and a defining characteristic of transactional writing is to communicate a message" (p. 123). And so, I rewrote the ending of this particular challenge and left a message for my brother from my father's perspective, knowing it could potentially alleviate his grief:

> And, for Dad, your efforts have always been more than enough. The pictures he took that day were for us, not him. Nevertheless, he knew you would hold onto your regret—and so, he left one picture just for you. (Revelation 6)

Last, when my family members sat down to read my stories, written in all their rawness and honesty, they too switched perspectives with me and were able to see the events from my point of view. Suddenly, a consequence I was not anticipating arose; our interactions with one another softened. Storytelling then applied a balm to our family's wounds, allowing us to heal and move beyond the death of our loved one together, strengthening our family ties post-loss.

Understanding the Grieving Community

When I set out to conduct an autoethnographic study, one of my goals was to be a voice for the grieving community, which I understood to be an oppressed population. Thus, I was determined to weave real, grief-illiterate interactions throughout the stories, highlighting their negative impact on the bereaved, emphasizing the need for grief education in schools. As I wrote about the insensitivities I endured, a feeling of disclosure through exposure emerged, carrying a reparative release of the destructive actions of others. Those unspoken cultural exchanges between the griever and non-griever that would have remained hidden, and potentially prohibited my social reintegration post-loss, were now out in the open:

> In an ideal world, upsetting experiences are transformed into stories that are shared with others. This process helps us to understand the events and, at the same time, alerts our friends to our emotional and psychological state. Such storytelling ultimately helps us maintain a stable social and emotional life. (Pennebaker, 2000, p. 15)

As my writing progressed, I felt as though I was bridging my thoughts to those of other grievers, sharing our common stories to create change. This increased my stamina to write out in detail every concrete example of hurtful language or inconsiderate action we collectively endured. To confront grief illiteracy, as the title of this book suggests, it was necessary to build an invisible relationship with other grievers through my writing, ensuring my words reached out and placed a comforting hand on their shoulder. Using my field notes as evidence, I worked hard to construct narratives written from my perspective about issues I knew were shared by many others,

> *But sadly, after the loss of my father, I would hear of many similar stories where apathetic, aggressive medical staff were encountered and basic compassion and bedside manners were lacking. I learned that we were not an exception; we were part of a commonly felt rule.* (Revelation 13)

To bring reliability, credibility, and validity to my data, I had to move beyond simply writing out my grief story and consciously expand to our community's grief stories. Hence, I kept my ambitions in check by selecting specific material that I knew would not be read as a one-off or isolated experience:

> *While grieving, some stood at the shoreline and ensured my safety from afar, some dove in and swam alongside me, and some refused to acknowledge the depth of the ocean, fearing they too would drown. And who landed where shocked me.* (Revelation 36)

I made sure my grief did not overtake the writing, that no specific person or establishment was identified, and that my words sought understanding, not revenge. The satisfaction of shaping the conscience of the grief-illiterate population and building stronger ties with the grieving community through my writing contributed to a feeling that better days are ahead for grievers—that a difference would be made, that we could move forward from feeling like lepers (Lewis, 1961). The stories, funneling my sorrow, became a form of service. Although Pennebaker and Evans (2014) state that "expressive writing doesn't need to be read by anyone in order for you to benefit from it" (p. 17), in my case, knowing that those who grieve could read, connect, and feel relief from my writing, enhanced my progression. As previous authors have noted, grief must be witnessed to be healed (Attig, 2019; Kessler, 2019)—and this form of witnessing was carried out through reciprocal exchange. To heal grief is not to force it into a conclusion. Instead, we break the heart fully and allow our love to continue to spill, openly sharing our stories and discovering the elements of relatability among them.

Designing a Blueprint of Grief

Storytelling provided the intricate structure I needed to explore the reasons behind my physical, social, psychological, behavioral, and spiritual reactions and responses to the loss of my father. Essentially, I was designing a blueprint of my grief. Rando (1993) states that complicated mourning can arise from "sudden, unexpected death…the mourner's perception of the death as preventable…and the mourner's perceived lack of social support" (p. 5), which I felt were all contributing factors to my intense bereavement. However, the more evidence I gathered in my writing that proved otherwise, the more I realized that his death was not completely unexpected, the illness was not preventable, and I eventually found the support I needed. As Pennebaker (2000) details,

> The beauty of a narrative is that it allows us to tie all of the changes in our life into a broad comprehensive story. That is, in the same story we can talk about the cause of the event and its many implications….Through this process, then, the many facets of the presumed single event are organized into a more coherent whole. (p. 12)

Although physically, I was left stunned by the outcome, the notes leading up to his demise repeatedly conveyed that I knew on a deeper, spiritual level that his imminent death was upon us. Bringing the stories to the drawing board, I had discovered and identified many subtle inklings that showed me his death was not as sudden and unexpected as I had perceived it to be. This went against my fundamental grieving belief that I was unprepared and caught off guard by his loss, as the content I wrote built a case for the opposite. Now, I could clearly see all dimensions and that I was an active participant in uncovering my father's prognosis, and I did have some control in the crisis.

> *Intuitively, I knew the time was closing in on us* (Revelation 3); *I paused to regain my composure and then invited her into the premonition I had just received, I think I will have to say goodbye to my dad soon* (Revelation 7); *I stared at his frailty. I had come to accept that I was witnessing his slow death* (Revelation 16); *I nodded but knew otherwise. My father's intentions were clear, he was ready to leave two weeks ago, he would not stay past twenty-four now.* (Revelation 27)

By mapping out an authentic blueprint of my grief, I gave my mind the concrete proof it needed to escape the shock of his death. This design reframed my mental assumptions, permitting me to assimilate and reconcile with a fact-based account of what had happened, and "once formed, the event can be summarized, stored, and forgotten more efficiently" (Pennebaker, 2000, p. 8–9). Gradually, the painful psychosomatic sensations my mind had created to cope with his loss dulled and left me. And, holding the stories as a tangible item in my hands, I reminded myself that assimilating and forgetting the trauma is not the same as forgetting my father.

Embedding Grief Work in Storytelling

Analyzing the stories, I quickly noted a resounding theme of finding components of grief theories and models embedded in my writing. To actively process grief, we must bring the unbearable parts of our loss forward and consciously work through them using researched strategies taught by previous grief experts. Throughout the data, not only did I reconstruct meaning in my life (Neimeyer, 2001) and relearn my place in the world post-loss (Attig, 2011), but my blueprint navigated my bereavement using the four process models I previously engaged: The Five Stages of Grief (Kübler-Ross, 1969), Dual Process Model of Coping with Bereavement (Stroebe & Schut, 2010), Tasks of Mourning (Worden, 2018), and Continuing Bonds (Klass & Steffen, 2018). Since narrative writing had become my vehicle for completing grief work, this pattern of using grief processing strategies to tell the story was crucial to my healing, allowing reconciliation to occur alongside the writing. Thus, combining effective grief theories and models, with the therapeutic value of expressive writing, with the coherent structure of storytelling—helped me to compartmentalize and process the painful details, freeing my mind from my tragedy.

The Five Stages of Grief. Initially, I thought The Five Stages of Grief (Kübler-Ross, 1969) were not as relevant to my mourning process. However, the more I wrote, the more I noticed I did cycle through these stages, most of which appeared in the anticipatory spaces leading up to my father's death, as Dr. Kübler-Ross intended (Kübler-Ross & Kessler, 2005). Surely, all five appeared in no particular order:

Denial—*That's just it, physically, he looks fine. Denial brewed between the both of us* (Revelation 28); Anger—*All of this anger and bitterness and frustration that accompanied my father's unknown illness bubbled and boiled over, creating a sharp I'm ready to go whistle for those around me to hear* (Revelation 9); Bargaining—*In an instant, my father's fleeting final days flashed before me. And I began bargaining* (Revelation 3); Depression—*The full force of grief knocked me off my feet—and, once I sat down, I was unable to get back up. I became severely depressed and uncontrollably anxious, rendering my physical body useless* (Revelation 39); Acceptance—*I could see the stage of life my father had reached, and slowly, I tried to embrace it.* (Revelation 10)

As noted by the numbered revelations, the stages did not present themselves in the expected linear fashion. They affected me randomly, and some, repeatedly. However, giving voice to these stages was therapeutic.

Dual Process Model of Coping with Bereavement. The DPM (Stroebe & Schut, 2010) more accurately portrayed my movement through grief and consistently appeared throughout the data. At times, I identified and navigated through the murky waters of the loss-oriented side, *How will I ever get married without you, Dad?* (Revelation 38). And at other times, I indulged in the lightness of the restoration-oriented side, *It's okay, Dad, I didn't want to let go of your hand anyways* (Revelation 38). For most of the stories, my patterns of mourning adhered to the oscillating function of this model.

Tasks of Mourning. Worden's (2018) Tasks of Mourning correlated with my writing more clearly in the last section of the stories, *A Year of Firsts*, after my father died. Here, I shared with the reader how I tried to accept my father's loss (task one):

> *I pulled out my cell phone, searching for the names of visitors who came to see my dad, and texted as many people as I could, informing them that he died. Almost uncontrollably, I hoped the more those two words flashed out in front of me, the more my mind would believe he was gone. That, I had just lost my father.* (Revelation 30)

I gave examples of how I attempted to process the extreme pain of my grief (task two):

> *My sorrow was too heavy; frankly, I had no other choice. Setting aside two to three hours every night to cry was the only way to find refuge, releasing my pain. And, as my grief squeezed out in tears, my brain processed the event of his loss.* (Revelation 35)

And, I described the adjustments I made to live in a world without my father, but also found a way to remember him while continuing my journey (tasks three and four):

> *Gladly, I light a candle, a symbol of my father's spirit, and leave fresh flowers, an expression of my love and reverence, in front of his picture—both acts acknowledging his ongoing role in my past, present, and future…through my grief-care, heavy acts of mourning have subsided, and smaller tributes of remembering have replaced them.* (Revelation 35)

By working through these tasks, I watched as the main character matured through her grief, and I more fully understood that I was coming to terms with his loss through my writing.

Continuing Bonds. Although my writing engaged with several grief theories, the most restorative writing came from deepening my understanding of the CB model (Klass & Steffen, 2018) and bridging this knowledge to form an ongoing relationship with my father. Purposefully, I extended our character arc beyond the final resolution of death, reinforcing in my mind that, on some level, my father is still with me. As I wrote the last section of stories, I began identifying strategies I used to continue our bond, and through the epilogue (Revelation 41), I summarized this wisdom back to my readers. Dedicated to my fellow grievers seeking ways to engage with the CB model, I laid out *five golden keys* that any person could use to practice and master the art of continuing bonds with their deceased loved one. By openly sharing my experiences with others, I fully grasped the concept that physical death does not equate to the loss of the relationship. This reinforcement of transcendent knowledge, viewing our bond as maintained and ongoing, instilled a great sense of peace that propelled my recovery. That, spiritually, I can preserve a sense of togetherness with my father, just as he challenged me to do, and this wisdom sealed my reconciliation with his physical death.

Strengthening Spiritual Health

The death of a loved one forces us to blindly reach into the metaphysical aspects of life, questioning the strength of one's faith, raising our curiosity about the concept of an afterlife. Yet again, storytelling provided a blank canvas for me to explore my interpretation of death, helping me craft a spiritually sound conclusion to my father's life. Using narrative writing, I successfully aligned my story of loss with my belief system, a significant aspect of healing in the Indian tradition. As Holland et al. (2006) support, "sense-making denotes the comprehensibility of the loss or the survivor's capacity to find some sort of benign explanation for the seemingly inexplicable experience, often framed in philosophical or spiritual terms" (p. 176).

Weaved throughout the stories, I used the metaphor of an invisible hand to symbolize my religious and spiritual understanding of a higher power that was guiding and directing me through the toughest parts of my bereavement, bringing visible light to the darkest moments of loss: "another element of this coping response is putting trust in God" (Tyson, 2013, p. 330). As noted in Revelation 36, I understood: *An invisible hand shepherded me through the thick of it all, preventing me from experiencing more pain than I had to.* Likewise, I brought forward my own understanding of destiny and fate, using different versions of the phrase, *it was already written*, on multiple occasions, solidifying that my father's death was beyond our control. By raising my spiritual awareness toward the unseen aspects of death, I was able to surrender to a divine process,

> The most favorable adaptation to bereavement is associated with the high attribution of sense to the loss, in the presence of low perceived benefit. It

could be that this latter profile reflects a pattern of meaning-making associated with "altruistic acceptance" or the ability to put a significant loss into a broader spiritual or secular frame of intelligibility, but without an implication of personal gain. (Holland et al., 2006, p. 185)

Writing that shaped a broader spiritual understanding of life not only strengthened my spiritual health, but it highlighted the blessings I did receive, which then had the power to overtake my sadness.

> *The spiritual knowledge my father shared with me in the early hours of this winter morning is imprinted in my mind, etched in my heart, and dwells in the core of my soul. His words will never fade. If I leave this world with one keepsake, I exit with this—and this is enough…When the intensity of my grief is heartbreaking, I refer back to his sound. And when my heartache is unbearable, my father's words reappear, ringing through my ears, reminding me he has already applied the balm to soothe my symptoms. While battling the relentless torment of my prolonged grief, my father's counsel saved me. (Revelation 18)*

Two strands of storytelling that strengthened my spiritual health were sharing our customs that bridged my father's path into the afterlife, and discussing the magical elements of death and dying that materialized before and after his loss.

Bridging a Peaceful Path

As explored in previous chapters, per Indian traditions, rituals are put in place to auspiciously bridge a peaceful passage for our loved one's spirit into the afterlife (Mosse, 1996). Culturally, attaining a sense of spiritual closure is necessary to lift the weight of sorrow off the griever. Although the reasoning can be reduced to transmuting sorrow into action so that one's physical body can find release, I found the experience of writing about these customs equally important. By chronicling the ceremonies, I more deeply understood the traditions I performed, why I performed them, and how they helped:

> *And when the seventh-day prayer concluded, something lifted…the materials required to sew ourselves back together post-loss are found within—rituals merely task us with committing to reach inward and pull the thread through the eye of the needle, so we can suture our wounds and recover…with every tradition I partook in, my cosmic understanding grew. (Revelation 34)*

Now, I had a record of the pilgrimage, prayers, ceremonies, observances, rituals, and fasting I participated in over the auspicious time of his spiritual transition. I could look at this large list of items and feel satisfied with my efforts of completing the spiritual requirements placed on my shoulders after he died. On several occasions, I mentioned that I knew we were following the practices he would have wanted, and a sense of fulfilling his unspoken wishes materialized:

> *The repetition of this ritual brought solace, a sense that he was leaving in the right way, a promise delivered through sacred words…I bowed my head but kept my head held high, strong in the knowledge that his faith was leading him safely to his next destination, a place more deserving of him.* (Revelation 27)

By solidifying that, as a family, we did everything in our power to perform the closing ceremonies of his life in accordance with our beliefs, my feet moved beyond the confines of chronic grief, and I stepped onto a more desirable ground. By honoring the many commitments and practices laid out for me, it was as though I had to *grief* myself out. Which, in the end, I did.

The Magical Elements of Death and Dying

As I walked alongside other grievers, a criticism arose around the little discussion had about the magical elements of death and dying and grieving, the metaphysical occurrences that were more closely examined in Chapter 2 as extraordinary experiences (LaGrand, 2001). Those striking, spiritually still moments that grip the attention of those dying, signaling death is near, or after their death, grab hold of their family members, sensing a loved one is near. As a griever, I existed in the *liminal* space—where my old understanding of life had fallen away, but my new awareness was not quite achieved—for an overextended period. While I was situated in this gap of mystery, mysterious happenings transpired. When these gifts first arrived, I considered them coincidences, or perhaps even a figment of my imagination. However, the more they appeared, the more I understood that magical elements of life after death can exist.

Hence, within the revelations, I tried to validate these spirit winks for myself and my readers. Gathering all of the examples I could think of, I explored these elements from my father's perspective and mine. In the first two sections, I narrated the mystical occurrences that surrounded him: initially, his inklings before he was admitted to the hospital; later, when he addressed his final journey, telling me he knew where he was going and *wants to go there*; and, near the end, when he disclosed the unseen visitors present in his room (Kessler, 2010). In the last two sections, I concentrated on the metaphysical matters that happened to me, such as hearing my comatose father call out to me—*Daughter, wake up* (Revelation 28)—right before he died. Or returning home to a house that had undergone supernatural adjustments: the biting cold room, stopped clocks, electric candles burnt out, or my father's plants drooping to the floor (Revelation 30). Lastly, the obvious exploration of the magical elements of dying came through disclosing the non-verbal forms of communication that survived past my father's death.

Although considered extraordinary, these experiences are common among grievers (LaGrand, 2001). Often, we hear the bereaved mention stumbling upon pennies, nickels, and dimes and viewing them as auspicious tokens received from deceased loved ones. And so, I elaborated on this phenomenon within my stories. I discussed how signs, symbols, and numbers, silently agreed upon from both ends, materialized at opportune times: *Daffodils, butterflies, and the number 14... when I needed his guidance or blessings, either individually or in combination, one of these three items would cleverly deliver a wink of reassurance* (Revelation 41). By addressing these aspects of living beyond the death of a loved one, my writing raised my confidence in my spiritual understanding of life, which, in turn, strengthened my spiritual health. Most importantly, identifying the magical elements of death and dying throughout these stories brought comfort, a feeling of continuing bonds with my father successfully.

Leaving a Lasting Footprint

Apart from participating in the religious traditions that contributed to my father's eternal peace, pursuing my doctorate and writing this book also fulfilled his final wishes—both achievements asked of me on his deathbed. In truth, though I am grateful for my ambition to succeed, the impact this work will have on my professional life is secondary to the lasting impression these stories will leave on me. The gravest part of losing my father is simply that I lost him. I will eventually get married and have children—and these new loves in my life will never have met the greatest love of my life. They will never witness the way my father cared for me or experience the unconditional depth with which he loved me. When I lost my father, they lost him too—and knowing this devastates me. But, by writing *The Revelations of Eapen,* using as much intricate detail as I did, I found a way to keep my father with me still. Truly, these stories were my attempt to preserve for my children my father's—*their grandfather's*—footprint, leaving a visible trail for them to walk in.

In memory of my father, I have not only shone a light on my suffering, but I have spotlighted the collective suffering of the grieving community: "In stories, the teller not only recovers her voice; she becomes a witness to the conditions that rob others of their voices" (Frank, 2013, p. xx–xxi). To know I have done something honorable with my pain and found meaning in my loss, turning my father's death into an act of service that will hopefully benefit the grief of others— leaves a lasting footprint of his legacy. This work is not merely a tribute or a testimonial to who he was, but an entire testament that he lived—that his pain and suffering and trials and tribulations did not go unanswered. I have borne the fruit of the tree whose seeds were planted and nurtured by my father's own hands, and this in itself has healed me. As I age and my memory fades, I will have my father's stories to look back on, read through, and hold onto. With these, he remains with me always, in every form, and until the end of my time.

Conclusion

When I first turned to storytelling to heal and move beyond the trauma of loss, I knew I would have to adjust the guidelines to target my suffering in bereavement. First, I had to identify my family's reactions and responses to grief and use their grief patterns to shift perspectives with them. Second, I had to design a blueprint of my grief, identifying the complex reasons behind my potent mourning. Next, I had to actively work to reverse this construction by embedding grief work directly into the content. Third, I had to strengthen my spiritual health by examining and validating my belief system post-tragedy and loss. Finally, I had to recognize how my grief work, written in the form of 41 stories, left a lasting footprint of my father's legacy in a meaningful way. It was only after walking myself through these four cornerstones of storytelling, embedding the expressive writing technique along the way, that I could confidently state that writing was an effective tool used to process my grief and support my reconciliation with loss. *Will every griever benefit from my findings or relate to my experiences?* Although grief is subjective and transforms from one person to the next and from one situation to the next, I do believe the overarching themes I shared throughout this chapter are far more common than our closed-culture discussions on death and grief permit them to be. Using this targeted approach to storytelling—with proper research, planning, and safety measures in place—impactful grief work can be carried out in the comfort of one's home, simply by putting pen to paper. And as grievers tweak the guidelines to fit their specific circumstances of loss, I am confident that a strong possibility exists for them to reconcile and heal from the death of a loved one using the therapeutic art of storytelling.

References

Attig, T. (2011). *How we grieve: Relearning the world* (Rev. ed). Oxford University Press.

Attig, T. (2019). *Catching your breath in grief: -- And grace will lead you home*. Breath of Life Publishing.

Bochner, A. P., & Ellis, C. (2016). *Evocative autoethnography: Writing lives and telling stories*. Left Coast Press.

Bochner, A. & Riggs, N. (2014). Practicing narrative inquiry. In P. Leavy (Ed.), *The Oxford handbook of qualitative research* (pp. 195–222). Oxford University Press.

Bonanno, G. A. (2009). *The other side of sadness: What the new science of bereavement tells us about life after loss*. Basic Books.

Bosticco, C., & Thompson, T. L. (2005). Narratives and story telling in coping with grief and bereavement. *OMEGA - Journal of Death and Dying, 51*(1), 1–16. https://doi.org/10.2190/8TNX-LEBY-5EJY-B0H6

Cacciatore, J. (2017). *Bearing the unbearable: Love, loss, and the heartbreaking path of grief*. Wisdom Publications.

Calhoun, L. G., & Tedeschi, R. G. (2001). Posttraumatic growth: The positive lessons of loss. In R. A. Neimeyer (Ed.), *Meaning reconstruction and the experience of loss* [Kindle version]. Retrieved from Amazon.com.

Chang, H. (2008). *Autoethnography as method*. Left Coast Press.

Doidge, N. (2007). *The brain that changes itself: Stories of personal triumph from the frontiers of brain science*. Penguin Books.

Frank, A. W. (2013). *The wounded storyteller: Body, illness, and ethics* (Second edition). The University of Chicago Press.

Frankl, V. E. (2006). *Man's search for meaning*. Beacon Press.

Freytag, G. (1863). *Die technik des dramas*. Autorenhaus.

Furnes, B., & Dysvik, E. (2011). Results from a systematic writing program in grief process: Part 2. *Patient Preference and Adherence, 15*. https://doi.org/10.2147/PPA.S15155

Gordon, R., & ebrary, I. (2000). *Dying and creating a search for meaning*. Karnac Books.

Holland, J. M., Currier, J. M., & Neimeyer, R. A. (2006). Meaning reconstruction in the first two years of bereavement: The role of sense-making and benefit-finding. *OMEGA - Journal of Death and Dying, 53*(3), 175–191. https://doi.org/10.2190/FKM2-YJTY-F9VV-9XWY

Holman Jones, S. L., Adams, T. E., & Ellis, C. (2013). *Handbook of autoethnography*. Left Coast Press, Inc.

Kessler, D. (2010). *Visions, trips, and crowded rooms*. Hay House Publishing.

Kessler, D. (2019). *Finding meaning: The sixth stage of grief*. Scribner.

Klass, D., & Steffen, E. (Eds.). (2018). *Continuing bonds in bereavement: New directions for research and practice*. Routledge, Taylor & Francis Group.

Kübler-Ross, E. (1969). *On death and dying*. Macmillan.

Kübler-Ross, E., & Kessler, D. (2005). *On grief and grieving: Finding the meaning of grief through the five stages of loss*. Simon & Schuster.

LaGrand, L. E. (2001). *Gifts from the unknown: Using extraordinary experiences to cope with loss and change*. Authors

Choice Press.

Lepore, S. J., & Smyth, J. M. (Eds.). (2002). *The writing cure: How expressive writing promotes health and emotional well-being.* American Psychological Association.

Levine, P. A. (2015). *Trauma and memory: Brain and body in a search for the living past: a practical guide for understanding and working with traumatic memory.* North Atlantic Books.

Lewis, C. S. (1961). *A grief observed.* Bantam Books.

Mathew, L.E. (2022). *The Revelations of Eapen.* DIO Press Inc.

Mosse, D. (1996). South Indian Christians, purity/impurity, and the caste system: Death ritual in a Tamil Roman Catholic community. *The Journal of the Royal Anthropological Institute, 2*(3), 461. https://doi.org/10.2307/3034898

Neimeyer, R. A. (1999). Narrative strategies in grief therapy. *Journal of Constructivist Psychology, 12*(1), 65–85. https://doi.org/10.1080/107205399266226

Neimeyer, R. A. (2001). *Meaning reconstruction & the experience of loss* [Kindle version] Retrieved from Amazon.com.

Olson, D. R. (2016). *The mind on paper: Reading, consciousness, and rationality.* Cambridge University Press.

Pennebaker, J. W. (2000). Telling stories: The health benefits of narrative. *Literature and Medicine, 19*(1), 3–18. https://doi.org/10.1353/lm.2000.0011

Pennebaker, J. W. (2011). *The secret life of pronouns: What our words say about us* (1st U.S ed). Bloomsbury Press.

Pennebaker, J. W., & Beall, S. K. (1986). Confronting a traumatic event: Toward an understanding of inhibition and disease. *Journal of Abnormal Psychology, 95*(3), 274–281. https://doi.org/10.1037/0021-843X.95.3.274

Pennebaker, J. W., & Evans, J. F. (2014). *Expressive writing: Words that heal.* Idyll Arbor, Inc.

Pennebaker, J. W., & Smyth, J. M. (2016). *Opening up by writing it down: How expressive writing improves health and eases emotional pain* (Third edition). The Guilford Press.

Rando, T. (1993). *Treatment of Complicated Mourning.* Research Press.

Schank, R. C. (1990). *Tell me a story: A new look at real and artificial memory.* Scribner.

Smyth, J., True, N., & Souto, J. (2001). Effects of writing about traumatic experiences: The necessity for narrative structuring. *Journal of Social and Clinical Psychology, 20*(2), 161–172. https://doi.org/10.1521/jscp.20.2.161.22266

Stroebe, M., & Schut, H. (2010). The dual process model of coping with bereavement: A decade on. *OMEGA - Journal of Death and Dying, 61*(4), 273–289. https://doi.org/10.2190/OM.61.4.b

Tyson, J. (2013). Turning a tragedy into a tribute: A literature review of creating meaning afte loss of a loved one. *Illness, Crisis & Loss, 21*(4), 325–340. https://doi.org/10.2190/IL.21.4.e

Van der Kolk, B. (2014). *The body keeps the score.* Penguin Books.

Worden, J.W. (2018). *Grief Counseling and grief therapy: A handbook for the mental health practitioner.* Springer Publishing Company, LLC.

Zinsser, W. (2006). *On writing well: The classic guide to writing nonfiction* (30th anniversary ed., 7th ed., rev.updated). HarperCollins.

Chapter 7

STORYTELLING THROUGH YOUR SADNESS

Bringing Grief Work into the Classroom

> One cannot improve education without a fuller understanding of mind, just as one cannot fully understand the mind without a fuller account of the role of reading and writing and literacy in general on human rationality. (Olson, 2016, xiii)

Canadian schools are witnessing an epidemic on the rise, as sources now suggest that one in five students are at risk of developing a mental health disorder (Kutcher et al., 2015). Consequently, a new wave of teaching positive mental health practices in schools has emerged. However, from the lens of my expertise as both an English Language Arts teacher, who reads deeply personal pieces of student writing, and a mental health support teacher, who listens to deeply personal accounts of student experiences, I have observed that some form of unprocessed grief almost always lives at the center of their mental health distress or problem. Therefore, it is my professional understanding that to improve student mental health, we must focus on student grief.

Student grief surfaces through a wide array of circumstances. Loss that materializes through death, divorce, friendships, health, identity, security, and social media status have all severely affected the well-being of my students, exposing varying levels of mental unrest. As previous grief literature has discussed, festering grief can lead to the development of mental health disorders (Cohen et al., 2017). Neimeyer (1999) also reinforces that inhibition of disclosure can become detrimental to our well-being, as "the psychological and physical burden of harboring painful memories without the release of sharing can prove far more destructive in the long run" (p. 72), possibly enabling at-risk behavior in adolescents who have not yet developed proper coping skills. Often, I find myself uncovering layers of stagnant grief that present themselves as behavioral issues, substance abuse, self-harm, eating disorders, anxiety, and depression. And although this chapter focuses on supporting student bereavement, the writing exercises can be tailored to fit non-death losses.

According to Statistics Canada (2016),

> It is estimated that 1 in 14 children will experience the death of a parent or sibling by the time they turn 18. 203,000 of Canada's 7.5 million children under 18 will experience the death of someone in their extended family. Almost 40,000 will experience the death of a parent or sibling who lives in their home. The death of a parent or sibling has been found to be one of the most stressful life events that a child or youth can experience. (Children and Youth Grief Network, 2019, para. 1)

Given the state of the global pandemic, it is safe to assume these numbers will see a significant rise, as post-COVID-19, grief is materializing in a multitude of ways, such as in hidden, ambiguous, and anticipatory forms (Canadian Mental Health Association, 2020). It is crucial that we expand our idea of meeting the learning needs of diverse populations in schools to include those of the grieving community, especially in the midst of a pandemic. Now is the time to address the phenomenon of grief in the classroom. Van der Kolk (2014) supports that "being able to feel safe with other people is probably the single most important aspect of mental health; safe connections are fundamental to meaningful and satisfying lives" (p. 81). Furthermore, having a solid community or social support system has been identified as an essential component of helping grievers reconcile with their loss (Rando, 1993; Wolfelt, 2003).

Since students spend most of their waking hours in schools, the tools, strategies, and resources needed to complete grief work should be available onsite. Bringing grief education into the classroom or embedding therapeutic strategies into the curriculum does not need to be an overwhelming or burdensome task. Grief work can be carried out by making slight adjustments to narrative writing assignments that students are already required to write, tweaking the way they write them. By taking initiative and using an innovative pedagogical approach to writing, we can provide students with effective tools that bridge proactive mental health practices and student bereavement. Thus, I strongly recommend that educators play a larger role in combatting the decline of student mental health by addressing grief and trauma in schools and giving voice to student suffering using structured storytelling.

Bereavement in the Classroom

> Children grieve deeply. Grief is an ongoing process that does not have a statute of limitations. Children do not 'get over' their grief but, like adults, learn to live with and adapt to the loss of a parent, sibling, or other loved one. (Cohen & Mannarino, 2011, p. 118)

After experiencing the loss of a loved one, students can suffer anywhere from normal to acute grief, depending on their circumstances. Yet, whether short- or long-term, grief disrupts a student's ability to learn, socialize, and integrate new experiences (Cohen & Mannarino, 2011). Teachers may notice that bereaved students socially withdraw due to their feelings of intense pain or sadness or because they feel isolated from peers who have not had the same experiences with death as them (Dyregrov, 2008). Death has prematurely matured them, segregating them from the unaffected innocence of their social circles. In more severe cases, physiological changes brought on by traumatic grief will affect their academic achievement, as bereaved persons can suffer from memory loss, frightening or distressing memories, confusion, avoidance, and disengagement from their usual activities (Cohen et al., 2017). Similar to my experiences, reading and writing can become challenging tasks, as most of the griever's energy is directed toward controlling the inner chaos of loss. Dyregrov (2008) supports that,

> Children may experience difficulties with attention and concentration. Thoughts and memories of what has happened will interrupt their lines of thought; increased anxiety leads them to monitoring their surroundings for danger or involves thoughts about the safety of loved ones…and sadness and grief may lead to 'slower' thinking and a lack of energy and initiative. (p. 38–39)

Teachers working with adolescent populations know their students are vulnerable to neurodevelopment changes that affect their decision-making and risk-taking behavior (Meldrum et al., 2009) and support them accordingly. Likewise, educators will be more equipped to reduce the academic barriers of bereaved students if they better understand the traumatized brain and its impact on the central nervous system. As Cohen and Mannarino (2011) suggest, "educators may be the first and only adult to recognize children's significant PTSD symptoms" (p. 120). Thus, teachers need to be able to discern and identify these symptoms to ensure their students receive immediate mental health support.

Students who suffer a significant loss view the world differently; they become exposed to secondary losses that materialize rapidly. Initially, the signs of trauma may be visible and understood. But as time goes on, chronic grief may be misconstrued, wrongly labeled as a learning disorder, or viewed as defiance, exacerbating their responses to loss through strict disciplinary action. To counteract these factors, bereaved students should be paired with a trusted adult who can help them develop effective coping mechanisms. Certain events such as field trips or school assemblies (i.e., MADD presentations, cancer research fundraisers, addiction recovery speakers, etc.) could bring up "trauma", "loss", and/or "change" reminders (Cohen & Mannarino, 2011, p. 121) that trigger their grief. Having a trained school staff member onsite could help eliminate, reduce, or possibly remove conflicts ahead of time. Providing educators with mental health training and grief education, covering the effect of trauma on student learning, increases the likelihood of bereaved students successfully reintegrating into their school community post-loss. But first, to move forward with this vital work, a foundation of compassion and empathy must be embedded within the school's framework.

Positive School Leadership

Murphy and Louis's (2018) Positive School Leadership (PSL) model developed out of an understanding that strengthening quality relationships within a school community was essential and that "school leadership is, above all, a moral and ethical task" (p. 3). The foundation of the PSL model rests on keywords like empathy, altruism, compassion, sensitivity, and purpose—traits that firmly align with the fundamentals needed to carry out grief work in a school setting. By taking a compassionate leadership approach, professional capacity is built to meet the intellectual and emotional needs of both staff and students, creating "positive environments in which human beings can thrive" (Murphy & Louis, 2018, p. 1). The PSL model argues that effective leadership includes the responsibility of increasing the emotional and psychological safety of a school community by securing student access to current, effective, and proactive mental health practices. Through leader-directed guidance, principals can effectively take the "psychological temperature" (Murphy & Louis, 2018, p. 96) of their environment and put the necessary supports in place by "paying singular attention to the affective and emotional needs of others" (Liden et al., 2008, p. 163).

Positive School Leaders commit to investing in the psychological capital of their community, "a cluster of personal resources that each individual can draw on to enhance his or her well-being and effectiveness" (Murphy & Louis, 2018, p. 92), and view these resources as equally as important as academic supplies. When addressing bereavement in schools, psychological capital would be providing grief training for staff, updating current grief literature in the staff and student library, assigning a supportive staff member to specialize in grief education and grief work assistance in the classroom, and connecting the bereaved family or legal guardians with outside agencies.

When assigning a staff member to lead the grief support role in schools, educational leaders should carefully select those who already feel a vocational calling or strong desire to support bereaved students. As Murphy and Louis (2018) inform: "Job crafting is deeply connected to teachers' (and others') sense of meaningfulness, and meaningfulness leads to increased job commitment and higher motivation" (p. 96). Grief support is not an easy task to take on, and so it should not be randomly selected or forced upon educators—an organic fit is best. As the designated mental health support teacher of my school, I found it beneficial to have received training in the following programs: Go-To Educator: Mental Health Literacy (MHL), Mental Health First Aid (MHFA), Applied Suicide Intervention Skills Training (ASIST), Brain Story Certification (AFWI), Social-Emotional Learning (SEL) training, Children's Grief Centre workshops, and Grief Counseling and Bereavement Support Training courses offered through the Portland Institute for Loss and Transition. Lastly, my understanding of successful grief support, although certainly not a requirement, would be that the designated teacher has experienced a significant loss themselves, bridging an otherwise existing emotional gap between the staff and student. Teachers are a great support system for grieving students because "teachers know the individual child…are experts in providing children with knowledge, more so than psychologists and psychiatrists…[and] are well-known and trusted by the children" (Dyregrov, 2008, p. 127). Thus, allowing educators to take the lead in supporting bereaved students in schools not only makes sense but is a crucial step in strengthening their mental well-being.

Addressing Grief Work in Schools Using the Art of Storytelling

As an English Language Arts teacher, storytelling seemed like a viable option to support grief work in schools because it can seamlessly integrate into the classroom and is an art form that students generally enjoy pursuing. Moreover, narrative writing is already a required outcome of the English Language Arts Program of Studies: "create oral, print and other media texts that include main and minor characters, and show how the main character develops and changes as a result of the action and events" (Alberta Education, 2000, p. 45). In the case of grief work, the story would be written from the first-person point of view of the student, who is the main character who changes and evolves as a result of the loss of their loved one. Even if students choose not to write about their personal experiences, the prompting of a fictional topic that everyone can write about has been found to have a positive impact on well-being: "Writing about an imaginary trauma in a deeply personal way was found to improve people's physical health almost as effectively as writing about their own trauma" (Pennebaker & Smyth, 2016, p. 162). In this way, private, ambiguous, or disenfranchised grief would not need to be shared directly. However, if the designated teacher can support the student to create a personal narrative, the healing that emerges from writing through one's own story of loss is powerful, as was shown in my study.

Tasks for the Teacher

Educators may choose to bring grief work into the classroom with a large group of students in a nonspecific way or work with identified students individually in a safe and supervised setting. Grief story workshops should be optional, obtaining both student and family or legal guardian consent prior to starting targeted grief work. Before a student begins storytelling, the designated teacher should know the story themselves by reviewing student files, speaking with family members or guardians, and having prior conversations with the bereaved child. The student's health history, personality traits, family values, and vulnerability must all be delicately balanced by the teacher. To prevent re-traumatization, students should not write about a trauma that is ongoing, very recent, overwhelming, or visibly increases signs of mental distress (Pennebaker & Smyth, 2016). Assistive technology should be made available for students with a physical or learning disability or who struggle to write by hand. In unique circumstances, the teacher may need to act as a scribe. In the latter case, I would encourage the designated teacher to find creative ways to engage the student with writing, such as using a fill-in-the-blank template, as verbal disclosure might not have the same therapeutic impact as writing (Pennebaker, 2000).

Educational leaders, family members, and staff should be aware of the grief story session times and be prepared to support students who may feel sad or upset immediately after writing. According to Pennebaker and Smyth (2016), "these negative feelings usually dissipate within an hour or so" (p. 169). However, extended assistance should be available to absorb any prolonged aftereffects of engaging in grief work. Apart from the designated teacher, the grief support team could include the school administration, teaching team, crisis team, school nurse, school or child psychologist, guidance counselors, health services, and family members or legal guardians, depending on the severity of the situation. The designated teacher should remain attentive to each student's physical, emotional, and psychological safety while engaging in grief work, ensuring their well-being is monitored throughout the writing and consistently afterward. All sessions should be logged using a 'before and after' mood assessment (conducted by both the teacher and the student) through basic questionnaires or screening tools provided by the school leader, who has already invested in various forms of psychological capital. If the child is talking to a grief counselor or therapist, teachers should connect and work in unison with them, as ongoing, clear, and consistent communication must be maintained with all stakeholders involved in caring for the child. Last, self-care etiquette should be taught alongside the grief work and upheld for both staff and students engaging with the story of loss.

Storytelling Through Your Sadness: A Seven-day Unit Plan

Whenever I approached storytelling as a means of grief work with a bereaved student, it was my job to read over what the student wrote, search for a narrative arc, support their ability to make sense of their loss, and find slivers of benefit within a tragic situation that was not yet visible to them. After each twenty-minute segment was completed, I analyzed the writing and formulated specific questions that led them toward uncovering the hidden, useful meanings found in their writing. Typically, these discussions helped students reframe their mindset and reinforced strategies, such as perspective-shifting (Pennebaker & Evans, 2014), to help them see beyond their grief. Then, I asked them to rewrite the same segment once more, but this time they were required to revise their language—pronouns, emotions, poetic devices—and include the sense-making and benefit-finding details into their plot. Usually, by the end of this draft, a visible, positive shift in their emotional state was seen alongside the emergence of a point of view they could not see before.

My recommendations for leaders and teachers who would like to support grieving students spring from my dual role experience within the education system, the analysis of my autoethnography study, and my knowledge of past expressive writing research conducted by professional authors who are experts on the subject matter. These three avenues have all contributed to the backbone of my approach to effectively embed grief work into storytelling. Like my self-study, students should evolve through a series of steps, educating themselves on the phenomenon of grief first, shedding light on their reactions and responses to loss second, and then using this knowledge to plan and write out their story last. To support educators who are willing to carry out this vital work, I have created a seven-day unit plan to bring grief work into the classroom, using a framework entitled: *Storytelling Through Your Sadness*.

Day 1 & 2: Pre-teaching Grief

Day one and two are dedicated to grief education and would benefit all students seated in a classroom. During this pre-teaching phase, the designated teacher prepares the student(s) by first defining grief, describing the relevant types of grief, and educating the class on the multidimensional ways grief can interact with survivors (refer to Chapter 2). Next, using age-appropriate language, the teacher should give an overview of a few current grief theory models, explaining their functions and leading discussions on the effectiveness of each (refer to Chapter 3). Younger students may benefit from reviewing simpler models, such as the Stages of Grief or the Dual Processing Model, while adolescents should explore task-based processing and meaning reconstruction theories. Junior and senior high school students are encouraged to independently research a chosen grief theory or model that aligns with them, stimulating active inquiry and engagement in the whole healing process.

Lastly, educators should teach students how to support one another through the hardships of loss using Wolfelt's (2006) Eleven Tenets of Companioning the Bereaved (resource available online), which create "conditions that allow the grieving person to embrace the wilderness of grief" (p. 21). By reinforcing ways to companion grief, we move in the right direction of reducing the rate of negative, grief-illiterate interactions in our society. The way to eliminate grief illiteracy is by assuring that future generations have the opportunity to become literate on the subject matter, and teaching these lessons through storytelling can be a solid route: "Grief education is quintessential to shifting our culture's antagonistic relationship to grief, and expressive, creative arts are an important part of this" (Cacciatore, 2017, p. 20).

Day 3: Planning and Preparing to Write

Each student will have their own subjective encounter with grief that evolves out of their family background, health history, and circumstance of loss. Thus, day three is dedicated to identifying their specific reactions and responses to the death of their loved one to prepare them for the writing stage. Before I wrote my self-narratives, I drew a visual *Grief Map* that helped me organize and label the physical, social, psychological, behavioral, and spiritual challenges that materialized during my bereavement.

The designated teacher can either create a grief map template, highlighting these headings, or students can organically shape their own (see Figure 3). The following prompting questions may be helpful:

Physical—*How do you feel since the loss happened? What changes in your body have you noticed since the death occurred? Do you have any new feelings of pain? If so, where? Is it worse at certain times of the day?*

Social—*Who supports you? Who do you trust? Have your friendships changed? Are you closer to any of your family members? Does anyone feel farther away?*

Psychological—*How do you view life now? Do you think differently than you used to? How has loss changed you or your outlook?*

Behavioral—*What are your daily routines? What is different in your day-to-day? Do you notice that you act differently from before?*

Spiritual—*Do you have any new questions about death and grieving? What beliefs do you have that are important to you? What do you cherish most about your story of loss?*

Figure 3

My Grief Map (2017)

Note. Moncy is my father's affectionate Indian nickname.

When having these types of conversations, a chance always exists that unexpected or concerning information reveals itself. If this occurs, grief support teachers should report urgent details to the school administration, parents or legal guardians, or Children's services as needed.

After sketching and analyzing their visual grief map, students can use this information to choose a grief theory model that best aligns with their journey. Once again, the designated teacher can provide students with a fill-in-the-blank template of the model, guiding students to use the information they brainstormed on their grief map to fill in the headings. For example, using Worden's (2018) Tasks of Mourning to organize student writing could look like this:

Figure 4

Tasks of Mourning (Worden, 2018)

How have you accepted the loss?	How have you processed the pain?	How have you adjusted to your loss?	How do you keep your loved one with you, while continuing your journey?

Note. Printed with permission from Worden J. William. (2018). Grief counseling and grief therapy (5th edition), New York: Springer Publishing Co.

By the end of day three, students have successfully built one cornerstone of storytelling by designing a blueprint of grief. By drawing out their reactions and responses to loss, and aligning themselves with a grief theory model, students have not only identified and labeled areas of their grief that still need processing, but they have also chosen a path of healing that could effectively narrate their story and move them closer to reconciliation.

Day 4: Organizing the Story

Using the details brainstormed from the day before, students should now organize their story by placing the events on a chronological timeline, restoring order to a possibly broken version as told in their minds (Van der Kolk, 2014). The designated teacher should prompt students to include as many specific, sensory details as they can remember, once again using guiding questions:

> What were you doing that day; how did the morning start? What were the last interactions you had with your loved one; what stands out most? What were your initial thoughts or actions after you found out; what was your first reaction? How did your family members react; how did they respond to you? What is something you wish you could change? What moment(s) are you most thankful for?

The questions should speak to the student and their specific story, ensuring their willingness to share and the sensitive nature of their loss is taken into consideration. By prompting in this way, teachers can begin formulating ideas on how to address the four cornerstones of grief stories within the writing task. When embedding relationship building, designing a blueprint of grief, strengthening spiritual health, and leaving a lasting footprint into student writing—a mnemonic device that may be helpful would be to remember the phrase: *build blue spirit feet.* The cornerstones do not need to appear in this order, but each fundamental should surface at least once throughout the writing.

Visually, students will now have a grief map, a grief theory template, and a chronological timeline to support their writing. The significant aspects of their loss found on each template can now be plugged into a plot diagram, forming the narrative elements of the story. Using a graphic organizer to determine the sequence of events will help students develop a coherent and intentionally constructed plot. As their ideas flow onto the page, the designated teacher should encourage students to identify a theme, such as revelations, personal to their bond with the deceased and pertinent to their story of loss.

At this stage, although the planning is complete and students may be eager to begin storytelling, the teacher should slow down so that students are eased into writing about personal traumas. To initiate the writing process, I suggest students take the time to create a metaphor that symbolizes their journey through grief: "One of the great advantages of metaphor is that it can compress a great deal of meaning into an economical expression or image, which can, in turn, be expanded by focusing on its elements and implications" (Neimeyer, 1999, p. 79). Through creating personal metaphors, students can warm up to the idea of expressing how they feel, using creative figures of speech. The metaphor can also serve as a point of discussion between the student and the teacher, allowing the student to expand their emotional awareness of loss by deconstructing their expression. The trained teacher should guide the conversation, supporting the student to travel deeper into the exploration of their symbolic comparison, paying attention to both verbal and nonverbal cues that signal when it is time to stop. Each step of the preparing, planning, and organizing tasks given to students before storytelling (days one to four) actively embed grief work along the way, allowing students to disclose their suffering in small doses before writing out the larger expressive writing task.

Day 5-7: Drafting, Revisiting, and Revising

Multiple days should be set aside for students to engage in *Storytelling Through Your Sadness,* and the teacher should plan for at least twenty minutes of assigned writing time per day. As Pennebaker and Smyth (2016) suggest, "writing multiple times is better than writing just a single time," and by spacing the grief work out over multiple sessions, "the between-writing breaks encourage a subtle perspective switch that a single writing session doesn't accomplish" (p. 164). In keeping with the guidelines of the expressive writing technique, I recommend a three-day model for storytelling, which includes drafting, revisiting, and revising the story. If teachers take a targeted approach with individual students, the writing days should not be in succession of one another.

Drafting. On day five, students should select specific events that occurred before, during, or after the loss that they identify as painful. The stories should follow their chronological timeline to continue restoring order, solidifying the mind's coherence of the events. If students are only comfortable writing about the loss in general, teachers should encourage them to start where they are. To begin writing, some students may require a story starter sentence:

That morning, I woke up and something felt off…

I remember the day like it was yesterday…

After I heard the news, everything changed. The first thing I did was…

Students should write freely about their loss without inhibition, judgment, or concern for grammatical structure, as the first draft is about moving into the *standard* approach of expressive writing, releasing their heaviness. When all of the student's thoughts and feelings have spilled out onto the page, or twenty minutes of writing has passed, the teacher should stop the exercise for the day and finish with a self-care routine such as debriefing, breathing, or light meditation (Cohen et al., 2017). Self-care routines and mindfulness activities are essential to neutralize or self-regulate tough emotions that students are attempting to work through. Thus, a planned, brief calming activity should begin and end each day of this unit.

Revisiting. Before the second day of storytelling resumes, the designated teacher should have read over and analyzed the content of the first draft of writing and left insightful feedback for the student, ensuring a plotline is visible. Using thought-provoking questions, the teacher should evoke sense-making or benefit-finding details within the griever:

> What emotions come up with your loss; how have you worked through them? How has loss changed your attitude toward grief or supporting a friend who has lost someone? How has your relationship changed with other family members; have you gotten closer to someone since losing your loved one? What values or beliefs do you have about death; were they met in your story? What are you most grateful for about the relationship you had with your loved one? How can you remember them or keep their memory alive?

By asking open-ended questions, the teacher is helping generate the details of the four cornerstones with students. After these discussions have taken place, students should be able to: build their relationship with at least one other character; navigate their design of grief, discussing the various ways they moved through the model; affirm their spiritual values and beliefs, deciding which parts of death they are at peace with, and which parts need further exploration; and, acknowledge the ways they have or will honor their loved one.

Teachers should monitor the student's writing—venting, blaming, or the overuse of negative emotions should be redirected into positive insights or perspective-shifting opportunities (Pennebaker & Smyth, 2016), as advised by the teacher. By reframing situations and guiding students to see multiple sides of the story, perspective-shifting could strengthen their social interactions with conflicted friends and family members, as it did for me. They can even confront hurtful or insensitive actions, reframing it as grief illiteracy. And once students have shaped some form of silver lining, they should rewrite their initial piece once more, adding new insights that form a well-rounded version, taking into account the point of view of at least one other character. The more versions a student can refine and rewrite, the better. This preciseness was integral to reconciling my loss—a gradual shift of grief's distorted perception to a more accurate telling of events settled my mind, as would be the aim in a clinical counseling setting. Finally, if the chance arises or is appropriate for the student, the designated teacher should support them to explore and write about their cultural death rituals and mourning practices.

By providing this space for students, they can record their customs, preserving their cultural traditions on paper. And, if students are willing to share their practices with others, they should be allowed to educate their peers on a multicultural perspective of mourning. In this way, culturally responsive teaching can support grief education and its goal of reducing grief illiteracy across diverse settings.

Revising. On the final day of storytelling, students should pay close attention to the actual writing of the story, revising the language, and editing the grammatical structure. In their final account, they should eliminate excessive details and bring focus to what truly matters and deserves to be on the page of their grief story—the words they use become privileged. And once the wording is intentionally revised and the sentences feel right, students should gain confidence in their healing, feeling proud of their *grief work of art*. As an added element, which I found to have immense therapeutic value, students could write about a positive, special memory they shared with their loved one, linking it directly to their story. The memory should bring the affection they have for their loved one, or vice versa, forward. By moving further inward, their memory will evoke beautiful emotions that acknowledge their special relationship with the deceased, validating the depth of the pain carried within.

Last, I recommend that teachers encourage students to include a picture of their loved one in their final draft. Attaching the image of the deceased to their story ensures the very person the story was written about is seen and kept at the front of the reader's mind—a three-dimensional form of witnessing. Images of my father that I used for my stories complimented each revelation, bringing my vignettes to life—*I saw how others would see him*—and by adding this creative component to their work, students can see the same. Here, the last cornerstone of *leaving a lasting footprint* is fulfilled.

The Challenges of Grief Work in the Classroom

When grief work is involved, foreseeable ramifications must be considered, such as reliving the trauma, experiencing emotional upheavals, having physical reactions to stress, and enduring cognitive disruptions. The grief support team mentioned earlier—a group of professionals experienced in trauma—can assist the designated teacher by working closely with students who display adverse reactions to grief work.

Another challenge will be the diverse learning needs of the students. For instance, English Language Learners (ELL) may have a harder time authentically expressing and moving through their grief in another language. In this case, I would suggest taking advantage of the technology available to us, encouraging ELL students to write in their native language using software that can translate meaning for the teacher. I would argue that, here, the accurate expression of the student's emotion supersedes the designated teacher's need for a full understanding of the text. Likewise, various learning needs—physical, cognitive, emotional, and medical disabilities—will need appropriate accommodations. As with any other learning task, the teacher should know their students, a thorough file review should be conducted, and the strengths and weaknesses of each child should be weighed and measured against the task at hand.

Bringing grief work and grief education into the classroom will come with its own set of challenges. *Will a seven-day unit bring justice to student suffering?* No. Time will be a challenge and the designated teacher should be given flexibility on how to implement this unit. Some students may need less, some may need more, and some may need the writing tasks spread out over an extended period. Nevertheless, I took the teachers' workload and the curriculum's constraints into consideration and settled on one week as a manageable solution for an immediate need to combat cultural grief illiteracy, keeping Laozi's wisdom in mind: *The journey of a thousand miles begins with one single step.*

Conclusion

Since the loss of my father, I have been consciously opening the door for grief work and grief education within my school system. Be it through conducting writing workshops for grieving colleagues or supporting grieving students in my classroom, the visible healing that stems from the grief companionship I offer motivates me to keep going. And the feedback from parents, students, and colleagues who have willingly walked through the door has been enormously rewarding:

> *No one has asked our child to work through this in school before, thank you; I have been attending this convention for the past fifteen years, and your session was by far the best one I've been to; You taught us about grief in class, and then I lost my mother and was able to face her loss because of your lessons.*

Often, I stop and wonder why grief education has not been a part of the curriculum all along, as we teach students how to procreate and grow their families. Still, we do not prepare them for when they begin to dissipate, and the inevitable opposite occurs. Yet, a strong desire to learn how to move through grief is evident, as the rising mental health distresses in students is a visible cry for help. Therefore, this book is not attempting to blur the lines between education and psychology; instead, it is a call for the community to rise to the occasion and support the bereaved—to bring grief back into the shelter of one's surrounding support system.

From the lens of an English teacher, *Storytelling Through Your Sadness* is a unit that can teach our students how to engage more deeply with their writing, shaping better writers of the future who understand how to produce meaningful compositions of the English language. When we channel our intense emotions into storytelling, the flow of our writing changes. Pennebaker (2000) supports that,

> The same students who would turn in sloppy, poorly constructed, appallingly spelled term papers or essay exams would write eloquently about their own personal tragedies. When given the opportunity in the study, the participants intuitively knew how to put their life experiences into remarkably coherent narratives with few spelling or grammatical errors. (p. 5)

As teachers, we should be advancing the *why* behind each writing task, designing and supporting the construction of therapeutic processes that support the alleviation of student suffering. As we battle the mental health crisis in schools today, I recommend using writing as a readily available and inexpensive resource that can help effectively process unresolved grief in students. As Olson (2016) affirms: "Writing is a technology that brings existing but unnoticed structures to light…writing has all the resources of speech plus a degree of consciousness not available to speech uninformed by writing" (p. 63). And when these unnoticed areas of unresolved grief are identified and actively grieved through storytelling, further mental health complications caused by stagnant grief may begin to decrease or altogether dissolve.

In his book, *A Path with Heart*, Jack Kornfield (1993) retells a traditional story of a poisoned tree. The first group of people that encounter the tree cut it down; the second group of people who do not wish to harm the tree build a fence around it; and a third person "picks the poisoned fruit, investigates its properties, mixes it with other ingredients, and uses the poison as a great medicine to heal the sick and transform the ills of the world" (p. 78). For me, this is what a solid, high-quality education delivers—curriculum that teaches our students to pick apart the ills of the world to find ways to heal the individual and collective suffering of others. This is what I have set out to accomplish through this book—a dissection, investigation, and transforming account of grief. We can fight the ignorance of grief illiteracy by shining a light on the problem and solving it through increased education. And we can easily embed grief education through different avenues in schools, such as health education, mental wellness curriculum, or English Language Arts. Once a greater emphasis is placed on understanding the physical, social, psychological, behavioral, and spiritual toll of grief on our mind's ability to heal and reconcile with loss—then only can we effectively companion grief, assuring that grief literacy overtakes grief illiteracy. Now is the time for a shift, allowing a grief revolution to come forward, pick apart what poisons us, and reinvent ways to heal.

References

Alberta Education. (2000). *English language arts kindergarten to grade 9* [Program of studies]. https://education. alberta.ca/media/160402/ela-pos-k-9.pdf

Cacciatore, J. (2017). *Bearing the unbearable: Love, loss, and the heartbreaking path of grief.* Wisdom Publications

Children and youth grief network ca | education support resources. (n.d.). Children and Youth Grief Network | Education, Support and Resources. Retrieved November 9, 2020, from https://www.childrenandyouthgriefnetwork. com/

Cohen, J. A., & Mannarino, A. P. (2011). Supporting children with traumatic grief: What educators need to know. *School Psychology International, 32*(2), 117–131. https://doi.org/10.1177/0143034311400827

Cohen, J. A., Mannarino, A. P., & Deblinger, E. (2017). *Treating trauma and traumatic grief in children and adolescents.* The Guilford Press.

Dyregrov, A. (2008). *Grief in Children: A Handbook for Adults* (Second edition). Jessica Kingsley Publishers.

Kornfield, J. (1993). *A path with heart: A guide through the perils and promises of spiritual life.* Bantam Books.

Kutcher, S., Wei, Y., & Morgan, C. (2015). Successful application of a Canadian mental health curriculum resource by usual classroom teachers in significantly and sustainably improving student mental health literacy. *The Canadian Journal of Psychiatry, 60*(12), 580–586. https://doi.org/10.1177/070674371506001209

Liden, R. C., Wayne, S. J., Zhao, H., & Henderson, D. (2008). Servant leadership: Development of a multidimensional measure and multi-level assessment. *The Leadership Quarterly, 19*(2), 161–177. https://doi.org/10.1016/j. leaqua.2008.01.006

Loss and grief during the covid-19 pandemic. (n.d.). Retrieved November 9, 2020, from https://ontario.cmha.ca/ documents/loss-and-grief-during-the-covid-19-pandemic/

Meldrum, L., Venn, D., Kutcher, S. (2009). Mental health in schools: Teachers have the power to make a difference. ATA Magazine, 90(1), 18–20.

Murphy, J., & Louis, K. S. (2018). *Positive school leadership: Building capacity and strengthening relationships.* Teachers College Press.

Neimeyer, R. A. (1999). Narrative strategies in grief therapy. *Journal of Constructivist Psychology, 12*(1), 65–85. https://doi.org/10.1080/107205399266226

Olson, D. R. (2016). *The mind on paper: Reading, consciousness, and rationality.* Cambridge University Press.

Pennebaker, J. W. (2000). Telling stories: The health benefits of narrative. *Literature and Medicine, 19*(1), 3–18. https://doi.org/10.1353/lm.2000.0011

Pennebaker, J. W., & Evans, J. F. (2014). *Expressive writing: Words that heal.* Idyll Arbor, Inc.

Pennebaker, J. W., & Smyth, J. M. (2016). *Opening up by writing it down: How expressive writing improves health and eases emotional pain* (Third edition). The Guilford Press.

Rando, T. (1993). *Treatment of Complicated Mourning.* Research Press.

Van der Kolk, B. (2014). *The body keeps the score.* Penguin Books.

Wolfelt, A. (2003). *Understanding your grief: Ten essential touchstones for finding hope and healing your heart.* Companion Press.

Wolfelt, A. (2006). *Companioning the bereaved: A soulful guide for caregivers.* Companion Press.

Worden, J.W. (2018). *Grief Counseling and grief therapy: A handbook for the mental health practitioner.* Springer Publishing Company, LLC.

Chapter 8

IN THE DARKNESS, A LIGHT

Concluding Remarks

The second way of finding a meaning in life is by experiencing something—such as goodness, truth and beauty—by experiencing nature and culture or, last but not least, by experiencing another human being in his very uniqueness—by loving him.

—Viktor E. Frankl, *Man's Search for Meaning*

After my father died, his loss crippled me, and using writing as my crutch, I slowly regained my composure and stood on my own two feet once more. When I finished writing the complete version of *The Revelations of Eapen*, the dark, heavy storm clouds parted, and the sun shone down on my face, revealing the path to my higher calling. The symptoms of post-traumatic stress no longer terrorized me. Instead, post-traumatic growth emerged, the "positive psychological change experienced as a result of the struggle with highly challenging life circumstances" (Tedeschi & Calhoun, 2004, p. 1). My desire to write these stories to express my love for my father brought meaning back into my life, and my will to live returned (Frankl, 2006). I could smile and laugh and effortlessly breathe, and gently, the joy of living resumed.

Although I knew that a positive shift in my well-being was surely felt, I turned to my best friend to gain an outside perspective as well: *What are your observations of my grief now that I've finished writing these stories?* Her response came through simple, but profound: *It's like you've been set free.* Writing did that for me; storytelling set me free. The unabated relentless pain I carried after the loss of my father was set down in words and released onto the pages. And once my grief found life on paper, it no longer needed to live inside me. My tragedy turned, shifting my perspective of it, reminding me of a beautiful life story I felt the utmost privileged to be a part of. *Can written first-person narrative storytelling be used as a tool to actively process and effectively move through grief?* In my experience, the answer to my research question is, unequivocally, yes.

To take the road less traveled in bereavement, I first had to separate my *fear* from my *grief*, or else, as C.S. Lewis (1961) posited, the two would become regrettably interchangeable. Next, I had to lean into the spaces of his death that made me the most uncomfortable and discover the hidden truths that awaited me. Then, I continued to tune into the second self—the one that gave me rationally sound advice—and carefully listened to the higher guidance offered on how to proceed. Last, I surrendered the need to carry the weight of my father's loss on my shoulders *forever*, as the death of a loved one is too heavy a burden for any one person to bear. The more I traveled down the rugged terrain of grieving deeply, mourning actively, and seeking new ways to reconcile, the more the tumultuous aspects of my grief flatlined. Naturally, I surrendered my inability to adapt and let go of my resistance to change. And eventually, the profound beauty of the story of my loss could be seen, even when life was not pretty. Wolfelt (2003) affirms that with reconciliation of loss comes:

> A renewed sense of energy and confidence, an ability to fully acknowledge the reality of the death and a capacity to become re-involved in the activities of living. There is also an acknowledgment that pain and grief are difficult, yet necessary, parts of life…the full reality of death becomes a part of us…the sharp, ever-present pain of grief will give rise to a renewed sense of meaning and purpose. (p. 146–147)

As I reach the end of this book, I see more clearly than ever that, even in death, my father's hand continues to grip the pen that writes my fate. Firmly, I stand on healed ground. My commitment to the goodness, truth, and beauty of loving my father has, as he promised, led me to lead a fulfilling life.

References

Frankl, V. E. (2006). *Man's search for meaning*. Beacon Press.

Lewis, C. S. (1961). *A grief observed*. Bantam Books.

Tedeschi, R. G., & Calhoun, L. G. (2004). Target article: "Posttraumatic Growth: Conceptual Foundations and Empirical Evidence." *Psychological Inquiry, 15*(1), 1–18. https://doi.org/10.1207/s15327965pli1501_01

Wolfelt, A. (2003). *Understanding your grief: Ten essential touchstones for finding hope and healing your heart*. Companion Press.

Chapter 9

THE MAN BEHIND ME

A Poem for My Father

When people compliment my intelligence,

they do not see the man who woke up early,

sat me at the table,

and made me memorize the dictionary each day.

When people compliment my wisdom,

they do not see the man who sat me at his chair,

lectured me on the power of knowledge,

and described the infinite possibility of this world.

When people compliment my words,

they do not see the man who sat me at his typewriter at age four,

placed my fingers on the keys,

and expected me to write.

The Man Behind Me

When people compliment my cooking,

they do not see the man who sat me on the counter,

revealed his secret recipes,

and made me measure the ingredients.

When people compliment my beauty,

they do not see the man who sat me on his lap,

wiping away tears caused by a culture that deemed me too dark,

reassuring me, I was his spitting image,

and showed me true beauty lies within.

When people compliment my confidence,

they do not see the man who sat me on a pedestal,

beaming with pride, announcing I was his daughter,

and how his dreams came true.

When people compliment my kindness,

they do not see the man who sat me in silence,

when I was unkind to others.

Life: To Be Given Back Again to Whence It Came

When people compliment my stillness,

they do not see the man who sat me by the trees,

and told me to learn from them.

When people compliment my patience,

they do not see the man who sat with me,

and showed me how to do one task a hundred times.

When people compliment my generosity,

they do not see the man who sat me with the less fortunate,

and taught me what is mine,

also belongs to them.

When people compliment my faith,

they do not see the man who sat me on the floor,

bowed my head,

and told me to give thanks.

When people compliment my strength,

they do not see the man who said "come sit with me" on that last night,

when he explained why I must keep going,

even after he is gone.

When people compliment my peacefulness,

they do not see the man who sits behind me,

resting his hand on my right shoulder,

reminding me everything is already as planned.

– Dr. Linita Eapen Mathew –

Afterword

Introducing the Companion Book:
The Revelations of Eapen

For a work such as Linita Eapen Mathew's, an afterword would have ideally need to be written by the central figure of this book, Linita's father. That, however, is not possible, and so I will do my best to say what needs to be said with the pride he would undoubtedly have felt at Linita's achievement. Not only did she catalog a pivotal period in his life as it affected her and those near to both of them, but she achieved what he would have wanted for himself, as well as for her, but was denied in his own case, namely a doctoral degree.

This splendid book is at least three important things. First, it is a literary work that characterizes the life of one remarkable central character with care and subtlety. Second, it is a result of research, though an unusual kind. Autoethnography is not particularly a common research approach, but a quite natural one in the circumstances and phenomenon that this work represents. Autoethnography attempts to catalog, understand, and analyze from the first-person point of view of the author, the cultural background of those whose lives and actions are under scrutiny. And, in this case, the primary person who so deeply affected the author is her father, whose cultural background was from India but who embraced in adult life the culture of Canada. Thus, this is a study of exposure to, and development in, two cultures that are very different but that overlapped in the lives of an entire family, including the author herself and the central figure of her researches. Third, it is a work relating to the crucial feature of mental health in these times, namely the problem of deep and paralyzing grief that can affect not only many adults, but many children in our schools too. The loss of a loved one, whether it be grandparents, parents, relatives, or school chums is all too common during the pandemic crisis that has affected us all for nearly the last two years.

As a literary work, Linita's companion book, her powerful sketches of *The Revelations of Eapen*, is an achievement of the first order. These 41 stories are an important addition to Canadian and world literature. In these sketches, her own crippling grief at the loss of such a remarkable figure and influence is laid bare for all to see. And so are her daily struggles to come to grips with the grief and to turn it back to her father's positive embrace of life as he found it, whatever the source might have been. But Linita does not stop there. Having achieved her literary goal to catalog her father's last year of life in prose and poetry, she then looks back on her cumulative story, her own 41 sketches, and the effect their creation had on herself as a means to her own healing.

As a research work attempting to understand what is humanly known about grief, its effects on individuals, and of possible approaches to its overcoming that never involves forgetting, Linita not only goes deeply into her own case and the researches of others but argues that one can learn from her multi-year struggle to cope with and go beyond her grief so that others might share equally in the benefit she, herself, managed. She plausibly suggests how her strategy of writing about her grief as a penetrating way to come to grips with it, and perhaps pass beyond it, while maintaining the strongest possible memory of what was lost, might be used in their natural educational context to the benefit of others suffering parallel grief.

The intensity of Linita's grief remains the same and is in no way less now than it was early on. In this sense, she did not cure her affliction. What did change is her approach to daily life and her own future. She is like a person suffering from an incurable disease who nonetheless does not any longer let that fact dominate her daily life in which each day has returned to being a positive opportunity full of future dreams and possibilities. One, where there is room for joy, love, happiness, and real accomplishment. Although not cured, she is healed.

I found myself touched deeply by her literary achievement, enlightened by her research approach and its results, and convinced by her suggestions as to how one might mitigate the deep grief of others in the context of our schools. It is a great pleasure to be a doctoral supervisor at any time. But it is an unparalleled privilege when someone like Linita appears unexpected in one's scholarly life. For this, I am very grateful, and I believe her father would have been very proud.

Ian Winchester
DPhil (Oxford)
Professor and Emeritus Dean
Werklund School of Education, University of Calgary

Author Bio

Linita Eapen Mathew, Ed.D., M.Ed., B.Ed., B.A., is a secondary English Language Arts and mental health support teacher from Calgary, Alberta. She obtained her Doctor of Education from the University of Calgary, writing an autoethnographic dissertation that explored the effect of storytelling on bereavement. She received the Canadian Association for Teacher Education (2021) thesis and dissertation award for her work's contribution to teacher education. Using her skills and expertise for service, she created and led numerous Grief and Writing Through Grief workshops for educators and bereavement support centers across the city. Her Master of Education (2014) focused on the benefit of embedding spirituality in education, bringing proactive mental health practices into the classroom to support student well-being. Her focus in education has always been to increase student achievement from the inside out—using targeted relationship building, spiritual dialogue, active listening, and compassionate writing exercises to reduce student suffering, which, in turn, raises self-esteem, resiliency, and grit toward successful goal completion and vocational alignment. Apart from being an educator, she is a writer at heart who has previously worked as a freelance writer and editor; and she is a symposium co-editor with the *British Journal of Guidance and Counselling*. In 2016, she completed her Reiki Master training, and she is the sole proprietor of PRANA, a thriving Reiki energy healing business based in Calgary. Here, she uses her understanding of spiritual education to support others through a holistic approach to healing, finding spiritual solutions to physical, emotional, and psychological problems.

CPSIA information can be obtained
at www.ICGtesting.com
Printed in the USA
BVHW091939040522
636049BV00004B/34